Gordon Griffin has been an actor for over 50 years. In the theatre, he has appeared in everything from Shakespeare to the first national UK tour of *Godspell*. He has also worked extensively on TV and in films, but he is best known as a multi award-winning audiobook narrator with over 900 recordings to his credit, ranging from Homer to Hilary Mantel, from Gogol to Chris Ryan. He received an MBE from the Queen in the Birthday Honours of 2017.

To Eileen Paulin Griffin (July 1913–May 2001).

Gordon Griffin

SPEAKING VOLUMES

AUSTIN MACAULEY PUBLISHERS™

LONDON • CAMBRIDGE • NEW YORK • SHARJAH

A CIP catalogue record for this title is available from the British Library.

ISBN 9781528989206 (Paperback)
ISBN 9781528989213 (ePub e-book)

www.austinmacauley.com

First Published 2020
Austin Macauley Publishers Ltd®
1 Canada Square
Canary Wharf
London
E14 5AA

20231019

So many people have helped me on my journey that I can't thank them all, but the following have 'opened doors' or 'gone that extra mile'. Firstly, I have to thank the lovely, supportive people at AM Publishing, especially Anna Cooper for her encouragement and advice. Thanks also to Stanley Bates, Gillian Bell, Simon Cox, Lou Gardey, Mike Hester, Derek Jones, Amith Lankescar, Helen Lloyd, Patch McQuaid, Sean Melvin, Ron Moody (not the actor), Roger Sansom, Simon Smith, Andrew Trepass, Aline Waites and Rich Woodhouse.

Special thanks to Hunter Gibson (for keeping on at me to get the book finished), Andrew Griffin (my brother, for endless support), Miriam Margolyes (for her generous comments), and especially Lois Brough.

The credit of the cover photograph goes to Chris Baker. Thank you so much.

And last but never least, thanks to Tom Dumbleton—my rock!

Introduction

The envelope looked very official. Too official. It could only be some sort of bill. Or bad news. I put it on my desk and ignored it. A couple of days later I picked it up and stared at it. I made myself an espresso and said: "This is ridiculous. By not opening it, I am putting off any bad news that it might contain." I took a swig of coffee and opened it. I read the first sentence. Once. Twice. And then let out a yell. My partner who was in the other room dashed in to see if I was OK. Was I having a heart attack? I handed the letter over. "Does it say what I think it says? I am not going mad, am I?" The letter was from The Cabinet Office and was asking if I'd accept an MBE in the upcoming Queen's Birthday Honours List. The letter was very formal and made it quite clear that the contents were top secret. I wasn't to tell anyone until the day before it was officially announced.

How had this happened? How had a fishmonger's son, growing up in the North East in the1950s, been offered such an honour? I knew it was because of my having recorded so many audiobooks – at that point over 750. And this was my reward. But how had that little Geordie lad become the person who had recorded more audiobooks than anyone else in Europe? How did I get to this point?

From Byker to Buckingham Palace? This is the story of the journey…

Part One
Getting There

Chapter 1

The teacher (Miss Carron, I think her name was) was standing in for the regular teacher who was on maternity leave. She was discussing what we would like to do when we leave school. This was a secondary modern school. Although I was well above average at English, I was hopeless at maths and to pass the 11+ you needed to be at least average at both. I failed. I was pretty bright and my teachers at junior school had great expectations, but I had been told very early on in my school life that I was useless at maths and it was true that, when I saw a batch of numbers, my brain went blank.

Miss Carron asked each of us in turn what we'd like to do when we left school. The girls wanted to be hairdressers or secretaries, the boys, bricklayers or carpenters. She came to me:

"And, Gordon, what would you like to be?"

I didn't hesitate. I answered, "I want to be an actor, miss." There was a very long pause.

"An actor?" she repeated.

"Yes, miss. Or a priest!" I have no idea why I said that. I just felt that saying I wanted to be an actor was somehow the wrong answer. I certainly didn't want to be a priest but I was in the church choir and I enjoyed the 'performance' element of that: being above the audience/congregation, wearing cassock, ruffle and a white surplice. We choirboys were there to support the priest. His costume was much showier and he had a better part. So, I suppose, I was thinking of being a priest as a variation of being an actor.

"A priest?" She was intrigued.

"Well, not really a priest, miss, (I suddenly was not going to be intimidated). An actor."

Miss Carron wasn't the only person to react in this way. The idea of a Geordie boy (yes, with a Geordie accent) wanting to be an actor in the mid-1950s was so unlikely as to be ridiculous. To start with, to be a serious actor, you needed to have no accent, to have a BBC voice, with 'Received Pronunciation'.

(This was before Albert Finney, Tom Courtenay and co made Northern accents acceptable but quite a long time before Geordie became acceptable or even recognised). I don't remember ever wanting to be anything else. From the first time I was taken to a pantomime, I was hooked. I didn't want to be in the dark auditorium. I wanted to be onstage in the bright lights. That's where the fun was happening. I envied the children in the show (the local dance school presumably) and wanted to be up there with them. There was one problem. I was painfully shy. So, when Buttons or Idle Jack called for kids to come up onstage, I was much too self-conscious to go up. The point is, I wanted to be onstage but not as 'me' but as a 'villager' or a 'page boy' in Cinderella. But from the first time I went into a theatre (and I was very young indeed), I felt an urge so strong to be part of this world and I never lost that urge.

Incidentally, the first panto I saw was *Babes in the Wood* at the long-demolished Grand Theatre Byker. According to my mother, they had real Northumbrian sheep onstage. I can't remember that, of course. Maybe she was pulling the wool over my eyes!

But why did I want to be an actor? I don't know. My maternal granddad was a miner at Brandon Colliery in County Durham. He was self-educated, highly intelligent and a vociferous reader. Not only did he have the complete works of Shakespeare and Shaw, but he could (and did) quote great chunks from the plays. There is no question that my mother inherited her love of words from him. She was a shy girl who escaped into her books (Charlotte Bronte and Dickens, and her beloved Keats). She also wrote poetry. She didn't understand music, although she enjoyed singing. She'd often say "Words are my music". Like her father, my mother could recite reams of poetry. If ever in later years I wanted to know where a particular line of poetry came from, I'd phone her up and she almost always knew. So, the love of words came from my mother. But where did the performance gene come from?

My dad had a pleasant singing voice and would sing in his laid-back style at Christmas parties but he had to be persuaded. He was not a natural performer. His father (who died before I was born) had once auditioned for the Carl Rosa Opera Company (or so it was claimed), but presumably, he wasn't successful because he ended up running first one and then three fish shops where the scales he had to deal with were rather different from those of a singer!

So the question: "Why an actor?" has no satisfactory answer. But there was no doubt at all that I wanted to be an actor and I never wavered from that desire.

An interesting detour: my mother's maiden name was Paulin. A name I'd very seldom heard. The only Paulin I'd come across was the poet, Tom Paulin, and he clearly was no relation as he has a delightful Northern Irish accent. I used to watch him on the now-defunct Friday night *Newsnight Review* show on BBC2. He had a wry take on things and a delightful twinkle. While other contributors were rather po-faced about, say, the Abba musical, *Mamma Mia*, Tom would slide further into his chair and say in his languid, drawn-out accent, "Well, I rather liked it."

One day, they were reviewing *Auf Wiedersehen Pet* (the series where the original cast got together years after the success of the original programmes). I was amazed and excited to hear Tom Paulin say that he loved the Geordie accent because his dad had come from the northeast! What? Surely, if his dad was a Paulin, there must be a connection to my mum's family. The name is so uncommon. I wrote to Tom and mentioned my mother's cousin who was a well-known clergyman in the area, whose first name I couldn't remember. Tom's reply was charming but he didn't know the answer to my questions. However, he sent my letter to his father who was still alive and lived in Northern Ireland. Tom's father was also the cousin of the clergyman and he was able to provide his name: Leonard. So, my mother and Tom's father were cousins. I was, therefore, related to Tom Paulin! And how appropriate that Tom Paulin is a poet. Words, words, words. Sadly, by the time I received this information, my mother was dead. How thrilled she would have been. Now, I watched the Review programme with a new interest and saw straightaway something I'd not realised previously: Tom Paulin was the spitting image of my granddad (my mum's dad) who died when I was fourteen.

I was born in Gilsland on the Northumberland/Cumberland border. I was the first-born child of my parents and they lived in a flat in the centre of Newcastle in a delightful street, Chester Crescent. As the war was on and as Newcastle was frequently bombed, some mothers were whisked away from the city to have their babies away from the bombing.

Gilsland is an interesting place. It's a village on the Roman Wall and was a popular spa in its heyday. A splendid hotel attracted visitors who'd come to take the rather sulphurous waters and walk in the beautiful countryside. In 1797, Walter Scott came (he mentions Gilsland in one of his novels) to 'look for a wife' and he found one! That hotel, eventually, closed its doors, and became variously a convalescent home and (during the war) a maternity hospital. It's where I was born. It was also the birthplace of the tragic figure 'Andy' Nielson, Ruth Ellis' son. Ruth Ellis was, of course, the last woman to be hanged in this country.

My dad was the second of five sons. My grandfather left shops in his will to the three oldest sons: Cuthbert, Bill (my dad) and Tommy. As my dad was fighting for 'king and country', my mum and grandmother ran two of the fish shops. So, as well as bringing up me (and later my brother), my mother was working a full day in the shops. When I became a toddler, I was installed in a nursery for part of the day. I loved it. I played the piano there and loved the singing and games. When VIPs came to visit the nursery, I'd be chosen to present the flowers. Music was to play a very important part in my life and even after I had forgotten the plots of television programmes or films, I'd remember the theme music.

Likewise, I can still sing some of those songs I sang at the nursery even though I've not heard them since and it's over 70 years since I sang them.

I was apparently a 'bonny', blue-eyed, rosy-cheeked little boy. I'd embarrass my mum, though, when we were on the bus. I'd smile at everyone who got on and say, "My daddy's in the army," and my poor mum had to refuse, as kindly as possible, the money the little old ladies wanted to give the 'canny lad'.

When I was six, we moved from our flat in Heaton (we had moved nearer to my dad's shops) to Whitley Bay. My mum, who'd worked in hotels in Newcastle and London, wanted to open a boarding house and run it like a small hotel. The house had seven bedrooms and pretty soon was open for business. It was a huge success from the start and for the ten years that the guesthouse was open, it was always full from May to September.

In those days, before we all zipped across to Spain for our holidays, Whitley Bay was a very popular destination for holidaymakers. During the 'Fair Fortnight' when the Glasgow shipyards closed down, thousands would descend on Whitley Bay and the Murray Guest House was packed. My mother worked incredibly hard but loved it. During the summer, my brother Andy and I lived in an annexe at the back of the house and having the house full of visitors didn't affect our lives much.

When I was eight, I started piano lessons. Before that, I'd just picked up tunes or improvised. Now I was taught by my Auntie Molly, a formidable teacher. I loved playing the piano but I hated practising scales, although fairly soon, I learned how to sight-read. While we had our summer 'visitors' in the house, I couldn't get to the piano to practise so had to pop a few streets away to my grandmother's (my dad's mum) where I could play and sing to my heart's content. One day, though, at home, when the guests were having their lunch in the dining room, I sneaked into the lounge to play. I realised, of course, that the diners would be able to hear me, so I always made sure I played a selection of Scottish songs to end my recital.

My mother was wary and tried to stop me but the guests insisted I play, so it became a regular feature. I had an audience, even though they were in a different room. And I seem to remember (even though I pleaded that I didn't want anything – and meant it), I made quite a bit in tips too! There's a theme here!

My first school in Whitley Bay was Rockcliffe Infants (immortalised in *The Likely Lads*. Ian Le Frenais one of the writers, was from Whitley Bay). I was joining the school at the age of seven, having started my schooling, before our move, at Sandyford Rd School in the heart of Newcastle. I was to be thrust into a world that was new with pupils and teachers who knew each other but didn't know me.

Before I started school, my mother, brother and I were invited with other parents to a performance by the children in the school hall. This consisted of movement and song. I don't remember the content but I do remember that it was lively and colourful, and that I wanted to be at a school where they did such things!

Rockcliffe School is still there, bold and imposing, and it seems to be doing very well (if Ofsted ratings are anything to go by). The infant's school was on the ground floor and the juniors on the floor above. And it was the 'juniors' that I remember so well. At one PTA meeting, the pupils put on a show. It consisted of a dramatisation of the song, *The Raggle Taggle Gyspies-O*. I was one of the three gypsies. It was my first performance in front of an audience and I loved it but I felt very aggrieve that Peter Taylor was given the better part of the Prince. Still, I was in it and I loved the experience.

We had an inspirational teacher in Miss Smith. She was an archetypal teacher of the period: grey hair pulled into a tight bun on the top of her head, tweed suits and sensible shoes. She was my class teacher in my final year at junior school so I was lucky that I was (even then) fantasising about being an actor (even though I didn't really quite know what being an actor meant) because Miss Smith loved music and the theatre. The school went to plays done by the Arena Theatre company in Newcastle, which, I admit, were rather dull, but we once (amazingly) went to the wonderful Theatre Royal in Newcastle to see a show about putting on a play! A well-known actress was the presenter and I remember one of the 'tricks of the trade' she demonstrated was how a fully laid dining table could be set up within minutes. The empty table and chairs were on the stage, the curtain dropped, and very quickly, it rose again, showing a fully laden table with people in evening dress sitting around it drinking and laughing. The trick, of course, was the settings were already laid out on a board the size of the tabletop which was simply placed on the empty table. To me, it was magical. I've not forgotten it. And I am still mystified as to why we went to see such a show and why a theatre company thought it would be of interest to Geordie kids.

Miss Smith was also the school's music teacher. Every morning, she'd get us to sing the second part of the song, *Early One Morning*.

"Oh, don't deceive me, oh never leave me.

How could you use a poor maiden so?"

She reckoned those musical phrases were more interesting than singing scales. Every morning, we would sing those lines. NEVER the opening of the song.

I was always fascinated by words. I loved English. I loved writing. I made up stories and plays, and wrote them in an exercise book. I wanted to do 'real' writing or 'joined-up' writing and before we were taught how to do it, I just joined the printed letters together. Suddenly, I was no longer just printing the letters.

I enjoyed the physicality of writing: dipping the pen into the ink and writing as neatly as I could on the clean white paper. At the time, there was a publication called *The Children's Newspaper*. It had a competition for schools, and selected pupils had to copy a paragraph in their neatest handwriting. I was chosen as one of those representing my school.

Our headmaster was well named: Mr Hardman. He was dour and terrifying. Or so he seemed to us pupils. One morning during Assembly, we were all sitting cross-legged on the floor in the hall. After we'd sung the morning hymn (played with enthusiasm by the aforementioned Miss Smith), Mr Hardman came to the lectern to address us. I was shocked and appalled when he said in his sternest voice: "Would Gordon Griffin please come here?" indicating the dais on which he stood. I was extremely embarrassed as I nervously made my way to the front of the assembled children. My face was burning and I was shaking with fear. Mr Hardman, still unsmiling, pointed to me and addressed his audience:

"This is Gordon Griffin…" (Was he going to cane me in front of all the school? What had I done that was so terrible?) "… He has made our school proud." I couldn't believe my ears. What was happening? He continued: "Gordon has won *The Children's Newspaper* handwriting competition."

I remember the huge feeling of relief rather than the pride I should have felt as everyone applauded, children and teachers alike. I think that the school received some cash prize but I got a rather handsome blue certificate. My mother had it framed. I still have it!

It was around this time that I made my first proper performance on a stage. As I mentioned before, I was in the church choir (St Paul's Church in the centre of Whitley Bay has been there almost as long as the town has). My brother, also a chorister, and myself, would be there for the early service (encouraged by our mother). For the early service, we just wore cassocks (the white robe was surplice to requirements!) but then we wore the 'full works' for the sung family service at nine o'clock each Sunday. We had to traipse back around six o'clock for Evensong. To make matters worse, we also were enrolled at the Sunday school in St Paul's Church Hall. One day, at Sunday school, I was saying the responses to the prayers when a jolly woman came up to me.

"You know all the words without referring to your prayer book." She seemed impressed. I explained that I was in the choir so yes, I knew them. And then she asked if I'd like to be in the Nativity play that was to be performed by children from the Sunday school on the stage of the church hall. The part was one of the kings. Would I? I remember even now the thrill and excitement I felt.

My grandmother made me a robe from an old red dressing gown and sewed faux ermine at the edges. A cardboard crown was painted gold with bits of glitter. I remember nothing of the rehearsals but I do remember being onstage with a large, live audience. It was thrilling. I must have been conscientious learning my lines because I can still recite my first long speech. I loved being up there under the bright lights, but of course after I'd said my piece and presented my gift of gold to the baby Jesus, I had a bit of standing around to do. On the first night, my family was in the audience and so was Pat, a girl I was trying to impress. When I wasn't involved in the action, I'd give her little surreptitious waves. No one would notice. Of course, everyone noticed and started to laugh. I still didn't realise until afterwards when my mother said how much she'd enjoyed my performance. "But, perhaps tomorrow night, you should cut down on the waving!"

Chapter 2

As I mentioned before, I was way above average at English but I was useless at maths (or arithmetic as we called it then). Every morning, after we had sung the second half of *Early One Morning*, Miss Smith would give us ten mental arithmetic questions to get our brains in gear for the day's work. Somewhere in the past, I'd been told I was useless at 'sums' and I had a blockage. I don't think I ever got more than about four sums right. Ever. I was still working out the first one while Miss Smith was rattling through the test. Useless. I think I was pretty bright but I was innumerate. 'Words' were my thing. To pass the 11+ exam, though, you had to be at least average at English and maths. Well, clearly, I was well above average at one and well below average at the other. Nevertheless, my parents were told that I would pass easily. The teachers were confident. But I failed! I remember being pleased at how easy the English section was. I even remember the story I wrote. The exam paper gave a sentence and we had to use that sentence to start a story. Mine was about a man leaving prison and adjusting to life on the outside. But that essay didn't save me! Michael Morpurgo wrote movingly recently about the humiliation he felt when he failed his 11+.I, too, was mortified and embarrassed and I know my parents were very disappointed. I do believe I was clever enough to go to the local grammar school, except in that one subject where I was useless. So, I'd be signalled out as a failure, aged 11, as I strolled around the town in my brown school blazer rather than the nice blue one that the grammar school boys wore.

It was tough for my parents who'd expected better. They'd even sent me to a coach to improve my arithmetic. It was a waste of money. I had a mental block with numbers.

Incidentally, I recently read in Peter Davison's autobiography (which I recorded) that not only he (Davison) but also Daniel Craig and Colin Firth were 11+ failures!

In my first year at Park School, I did at least get a good part in the school play. The director and writer was a teacher, Douglas Maitland, who was involved in drama in the county.

It was an interesting play about a teacher taking her pupils around a theatre where a company is rehearsing a production, Shaw's *St Joan*. There is a drama going on offstage as the temperamental director (played by Sammy Padmore – who later went on to write plays) realises that the actress playing Joan can't perform. The teacher takes over with great success. So, the second part of the play (which had many titles but ended up being called *Amateurs? How interesting!*) is the trial scene from Shaw's play. Sandra Wright (I think that was her name) was astonishing as Joan. I remember all these years later the power of her performance. I played the sympathetic Brother Martin. I was in my element.

I devoured plays. In those far-off days, the Whitley Bay library was in a series of rooms above the bus station in the centre of the town. As soon as I was old enough, I became a member and was so proud of my library card. I felt so grown-up. I even recall the first book I took out – *Alice through the Looking Glass*, a book I was to produce in audiobook form many years later. But it was the 'plays' section I devoured. I read every play I could get my hands on. I also borrowed music scores, mostly of musicals. I couldn't wait to rush home and play through the songs or act out the plays for my own pleasure. But I knew that that wasn't enough. I wanted an audience.

I had a puppet theatre, with an assortment of puppets. I'd make up plays using the puppets, practicing the different voices. I painted scenery. I made up songs. I was ready to give a performance for my friends. I went around telling my neighbours and friends that I'd be giving a performance in the annexe of our house. I set out enough seating, and even bought bars of chocolate and packets of sweets and crisps to sell before and after the show. I was all set up. All I needed to do now was to wait for my friends and neighbours to arrive at the appointed time to see the show. I waited. And waited. And waited. Not one person turned up. I even went dashing around to chase up friends who lived nearby. But no one came. Of course, I was very disappointed.

My mother was very sympathetic. I think for the first time she took my passion for the theatre and for performing seriously. She recognised that if I wanted to be an actor then I needed to do something about my Geordie accent. She contacted an elocution teacher who lived a few streets away – Sylvia Blair – and, after a meeting with her, I enrolled.

Miss Blair was a very attractive woman in the 20s. Her classes were held in a room on the first floor of her parents' terraced house in (appropriately) Gordon Square. The room was bright and empty of all but basic furniture, and the walls were covered with her certificates and diplomas. I liked her from the start. I soon became her star pupil and when she had performances in the local church halls, I'd get the best scenes or the most telling poems to perform.

The classes always started with me having to read a list of words. I soon learned to pronounce pass (like pahs) and not with a flat 'a' to rhyme with 'crass'. I became bilingual; Geordie and non-Geordie! Of course, I couldn't talk about having a 'bahth' with my schoolmates. I'd be lynched! It was 'bath' to rhyme with Kath. Slowly, I was able to talk quite naturally without the accent, although the accent was still there under the surface. I imagine if you are English but have grown up with a French mother and speak both languages from being a baby, then that is what I was like with my Geordie.

Quite soon, I was being entered for national exams in Acting and Verse Speaking. I always received high marks and my mother didn't know what to do with all the certificates I received. I was pleased about the prizes only because they so pleased my mother and Miss Blair.

I was always a little envious of the actor, Jeremy Spenser. He was a similar age to me and he played all the parts I wanted to play onstage in London's West End and on film. He had been playing the boy king in Terence Rattigan's comedy, *The Sleeping Prince*, that starred Vivien Leigh and her then husband, Laurence Olivier. Miss Blair heard that one of the top amateur companies in the northeast was doing a production of it in Newcastle and encouraged me (I didn't need much encouragement!) to go and read for the Jeremy Spenser part.

In the meantime, my grandmother had read in the local paper that the director of the nearby weekly repertory theatre company at Tynemouth was looking for local child actors to be in a play set in a public school. The play was *Housemaster* by Ian Hay. I went to meet the director, Douglas Emery, and read for him in his tiny dressing room (no more than a cupboard) backstage at the Plaza Theatre. I remember that wonderful backstage smell of paint and sawdust and cigarette smoke and disinfectant. It was magical.

I read for the boy king for the amateur company in Newcastle. There were lots of others for the role and I remember stumbling over the words as I read. I was nervous. I was sure I'd not get the part.

Sylvia Blair phoned me up excitedly to say that they wanted me to do the Rattigan. Just before she'd called, I'd taken a call from Douglas Emery, the Tynemouth director, who wanted me to play the main boy, Bimbo Farringdon, in *Housemaster*. Sylvia was adamant. I should do *The Sleeping Prince*. But in my mind, there was no contest. Tynemouth was a professional company. I'd be playing a very good part with real live actors – and I was to get paid £1 a week. That's was £2 in total. One week's rehearsal and one week playing. It was to be done in the Easter holiday so the school couldn't object.

So in April 1956, the curtain went up on me as Bimbo Farringdon. I was a professional actor. I would never look back. It was the most exciting couple of weeks of my life so far. I loved the rehearsal, the learning of the lines, the getting on the bus at the top of my street and getting off at the stage door of the imposing Plaza Theatre overlooking the sea. I was an actor!

The cast was so nice to me. Friendly and warm and helpful. This was really my first time on a proper stage – and I was a professional! It was a heady time. I was dizzy with the excitement of it all. Even the school made a fuss when I returned after the Easter break. There was an article in the local paper about me. Friends, family and teachers came to support me. Even Sylvia came, although she still thought I ought to have done *The Sleeping Prince*!

Douglas Emery was pleased as I had received a couple of good reviews and later that year (again to coincide with the school holidays), I received my second part. This time, I was a newsboy. Not much to do. But I didn't care. I was welcomed back. I was part of the family.

Although it was a weekly rep company, the standard of acting and production was very good. I went to the late afternoon matinee every Saturday and often went backstage to see my colleagues. It all felt very grown up.

Later, I re-joined the company to do a pantomime and then a farce. It was at that point that my headmaster put his foot down. I must stop the 'play-acting' and get down to school work!

In the third year at Park School, a new teacher joined the staff, Mr Turnbull. He was the English teacher and was particularly interested in drama. One day, we had a break from lessons and could read whatever book we wanted. At one point, he strolled round the classroom to see what we were reading. I was reading *Under Milk Wood*. He seemed surprised.

"Are you actually reading this?" he'd asked, which I thought was an odd question. I told him that I certainly was.

We had an hour's lesson every week that was called Drama. Quite early on, he asked me to perform something during the hour. I got some malleable friends together and we put on a play. It was a success (I'd made sure there were a lot of jokes in it) and, from that day on, the Drama hour was mine.

I still find it incredible that Mr Turnbull allowed me to do that. Too lazy to work out what to do himself? I really don't think so. It was wonderful experience for me. I always played the lead (of course) and I wrote the plays (mostly improvised, there wasn't time to write scripts or learn lines), and I made sure they were funny, often pinching gags from Worker's Playtime on the radio which I used to listen to during my school lunchbreaks at home.

In 2015, I was giving a talk about my career as an audiobook reader to a (thankfully) packed Whitley Bay Library audience. The library was no longer a few rooms above the bus station but a smart new glass building. The talk (which by then was tried and tested) went very well. I had friends and family in the audience, and afterwards, they gathered round to chat and ask questions.

I knew an old school pal, whom I had not seen for years, was coming so I had brought some school photos with me to show him. Then, behind the group crowding around the table, I saw a small elderly man hovering shyly in the background. I knew at once who it was, even after nearly 60 years. It was Mr Turnbull. I leapt up to shake his hand. He was all smiles. It was so wonderful to see him. Coincidentally, a couple of the school photos I'd brought with me had him in them so I showed him and his wife pictures of himself that he'd not seen before. I asked him why he'd let me have the Drama hour to do as I wished. It still mystified me. He seemed surprised by the question.

"But why wouldn't I? You did it so well…"

I was still mystified. But, of course, it was wonderful for me. And (as they told me years later) my fellow-pupils enjoyed those sessions too.

Talking to my school friends all those years later after my talk, there was one common thread. They all knew that I would make a success in the theatre. That was surprising to hear. But heartening somehow. I knew it myself but it was interesting that others felt the same. Especially given the time and the place and my background. Actors lived in London. They spoke posh. They didn't live in the northeast and have Geordie accents.

In all the excitement of seeing Mr Turnbull again, I didn't get his contact details. Or a photo on my phone. But I was so happy to be able to tell him face to face how important a part he had played in my life at that time and how important his encouragement was when all the other teachers and the headmaster thought I was wasting my time and should be preparing for a life outside school where I would get a proper job!

A few months ago, I got a Friend's Request on Facebook. It was from Mr Turnbull. I was thrilled to be in touch with him again.

Chapter 3

Despite the reluctance of my headmaster, I went on to do five plays at Tynemouth and a play at the Jesmond Playhouse, a fortnightly rep near the centre of Newcastle. It was a charming theatre, and in later life, became the Flora Robson Theatre named after Dame Flora, a respected and largely forgotten actress who came from the area. Now, sadly, Dame Flora and her theatre are gone.

Many years ago I met Dame Flora. I was playing at the Gardner Centre Theatre at the University of Sussex. Dame Flora, who lived in Brighton, came to see the play I was in She looked anything but a successful actress with her rather dodgy wig and dowdy clothes. There was nothing at all starry about her. But when she started to speak... that beautiful deep and rich voice was unmistakable. I'll never forget how charming and courteous she was.

After my stint at the Jesmond Playhouse, I was approached by the director of the Theatre Club, a very successful amateur group in Whitley Bay. Would I play a small part in a play by Jean Anouilh? Sylvia Blair had recommended me and the lady doing the asking seemed to know of me. It was to be during the summer holidays and I knew that I really had to study as I had exams coming up. And the part was small. I said no. She pleaded with me to do it. Really pleaded! So I reluctantly agreed.

It was a thoroughly miserable experience. Whereas the professional actors I'd worked with in rep had been very encouraging and friendly to me, no one even spoke to me when I arrived at the first rehearsal at the Theatre Club. There was some tension, I'd gathered, between the leading actresses and the atmosphere was not a happy one. It wasn't fun. This was in effect my first experience of working with an amateur company. Later, I had a lovely time with the Whitley Bay Jewish Drama Group playing the young gentile Cockney lad in Yvonne Mitchell's play *The Same Sky*. It was playing in that production that I met Ruth Caleb who went on to become one of the most successful and decorated TV producers at the BBC.

The only other non-professional job was my first musical, *White Horse Inn*. A year after I'd made my professional début at Tynemouth Rep, I was asked to read for the role of Karl in the show for the Tynemouth Operatic Society. Karl was the waiter at the eponymous inn and it was a delightful part that required no singing. Don't get me wrong, I enjoyed singing, but in those days, you were either an actor or a song-and-dance man. I was very much the former. Little did I know that a couple of decades later, that was to change and I'd find myself performing regularly in musical theatre.

I can't imagine *White Horse Inn* being done now. It's very old-fashioned and schmaltzy but the music is rather wonderful. Pure operetta. Oddly enough, the most famous song from the score, *Goodbye, I wish you all a last goodbye*, is the one I like the least.

I arrived for my first rehearsal and entered the school hall where we were to rehearse. Some chorus members were already rehearsing a song from the show – glorious harmonies and all. I was captivated. I'd never heard anything like it. I stood transfixed. This was my first experience of musical theatre – and I was hooked.

The show played on the vast stage of a cinema in North Shields, the first time I'd played on a full-sized stage and with a full orchestra. I had a wonderful time and relished my role. The audience loved the show and the reviews were great. One said:

"Gordon Griffin is delightful as Karl, the young waiter. He's as at home on the stage as a chef is in his kitchen. Kind words because he is so young? Not a bit of it!"

As you can imagine, I was thrilled with this review. I was 14 years old but I already knew that the reviewer was right. I 'was' at home on the stage. It was where I wanted to be. It was where I 'had' to be!

My headmaster wasn't too enthusiastic about me 'messing around' with theatre work when I should be studying. But he had no control over my summer holiday activities. We (as a family) didn't go on holiday. My dad worked in his shops and only had the odd bank holiday off and my mother, of course, was running her boarding house. But we were living in Whitley Bay. People came from all over Scotland and the north of England to holiday there and we lived there. We didn't need to go anywhere else.

A few years after *White Horse Inn*, some like-minded friends were inveigled by me to put on a show ourselves. I suppose my inspiration came from *The Blue Door Venture* books of Pamela Brown about a group of friends who take over an old church hall and put on plays there. I intended to do the same. So, with Ian, Sheena and Michael (school pals who were interested in the theatre), we hired the Livingstone Hall in Whitley Bay and put on three one-act plays. We directed and acted in them, and we called ourselves, rather grandly, The Youth Dramatic Society. Surprisingly, people turned up. We'd had proper programmes printed and tickets, and the plan was to make this a regular event.

I see from the programme that our next production was to be the John van Druten play, *Bell, Book and Candle*. That didn't happen. But we did have quite a success with our one-act plays, although the second play (I directed but didn't appear in) was set in a park. A man is sitting there and a young woman joins him. They have a conversation and when the woman goes, the man feels around on the ground and finds his white stick. He is blind. And that's supposed to be a shock to the audience. But I am afraid our audience roared with laughter.

The final play had Ian and I as lighthouse-keepers trapped 'like rats in a cage' on the island where the lighthouse is, by terrible storms. Ron did wonderful work with his tape-recorder in the wings, providing terrible storm noises and as musical accompaniment towards the end, as it was clear we

31

were doomed, he played in *The Ride of the Valkyries* very loudly. If we forgot our lines, we'd just yell, "We're trapped! Like rats in a cage!" All very dramatic but the audience cheered us to the rafters. We got lovely reviews and one said that our group should be encouraged. It was a huge logistical and not particularly cheap venture so that that evening of one-act plays was the beginning and the end of The Youth Dramatic Society.

In 1959, my mother turned her 'guesthouse' into flats and decided to go back into the catering business. She'd run successful dining rooms in hotels in London and Newcastle. In fact, it was while she was a waitress at the Queen's Hotel in Whitley Bay that she met my dad. His aunt ran the hotel and he lived with his mother in the next street. My mother enjoyed the work and was very good at it. She enjoyed the social side of it, although not necessarily the long hours. Christmas Day, for example, was a busy time for her, and my brother and I had to wait to celebrate our Christmases until she came home in the evening.

The boss of this hotel was an 'angel' – in one sense only. He put money into plays and he had directed amateur productions in Whitley Bay. He knew a lot of performers and a lot of big theatre names stayed at his hotel. He convinced my mother that I should be in London as there was no work for a young actor in Whitley Bay. He would arrange for me to take a letter of introduction to a successful London agent he knew. I was 16 going on 13! I certainly was 'innocent as a rose' (as the song says). Well, fairly innocent, and the idea of me traipsing around London on my own was a non-starter as far as my mum was concerned. I had other ideas!

My Auntie Helen and Uncle Arthur (no relations, just friends of my mother's) lived in Edgware, north of London. Would they put me up until I found somewhere permanent or, better still, until I got bored or homesick or both and wanted to come home? Reluctantly, they agreed. My mother was upset but I was determined. I would go to London.

It was awful waving goodbye to my mum and brother who stood tearfully on Newcastle Central station. I was feeling unbearably sad. I knew I'd miss them and home very much. But this was the chance I had been waiting for. I had to take it!

Initially, Helen and Arthur, who had no children, were friendly and encouraging. But after a couple of weeks, they were leaving notices by the phone of bed and breakfast hotels and hostels that I could, perhaps, move into!

My mother came down to London. It was obvious I couldn't stay in Edgware. I don't blame Helen and Arthur. They didn't know how to deal with a 16-year-old whose only conversation was the theatre!

We found a place for me in Canfield Gardens in West Hampstead (by an amazing coincidence, it's the street, though not the house, where I now live). Mrs Homewood was a kind-hearted Scots lady who was also a wonderful cook. She had a houseful of random young men, mostly pretty rough. But she liked me because she had three daughters who went to stage school so we all spoke the same language.

I made an appointment to meet the agent and took along my letter of introduction. This agent was pretty high-powered and impressive. Around his office walls were black and white photos of his clients; some very famous!

I'd not been with him long when he got me a job in the comedy about lawyers – *Brothers in Law*. It was to play at a theatre in Bournemouth and then do a short tour ending at the massive Hippodrome Theatre in Bristol.

One day, before I was due to head for Bournemouth and rehearsals, I got a call from him to say that there was the possibility of being whisked off to do a day's shoot on a commercial being filmed in the Caribbean. I was thrilled. A commercial? That meant money and glamour and travel. I was to go to his flat in South Kensington that evening to discuss it! Yes, I told you, I was naïve.

I got to his flat. Wonderful cooking smells came from the kitchen. He gave me a large glass of wine. Wow! This powerful agent was entertaining 'me'. He told me that in his bedroom on the bed were a selection of swimsuits, one of which I'd wear in the commercial. Yes, even though now I was getting suspicious, I tried them on. He selected his favourite, then told me to get dressed and come downstairs and have dinner. Of course, he pounced on me. I was polite but escaped unscathed. It was a very hard lesson to learn. I was shocked that he had tried to seduce me – he was my agent, for god's sake! But my main emotion was utter disappointment that there was no commercial. There would be no Caribbean trip. I was mortified.

But I did the tour which was fairly unmemorable. It wasn't a success. The play was small-scale and was completely lost in the huge theatres we were playing.

I found another agent, and before long, was at Colchester rep (before they built the new theatre) where I was to play in *Housemaster* again. This time, one of the other boys. Although I looked much younger than I was, I was a bit too old to play my original part.

Following *Housemaster*, I played Young Scrooge in *A Christmas Carol*. It was a friendly company. I stayed in lovely digs in Marks Tey for the first play (we were rehearsing in the day) but when we were just playing *A Christmas Carol*, I commuted to and from Canfield Gardens.

My best friend in the company was Ronald Lacey. Ronnie lived in Harrow-on-the-Hill (further north than West Hampstead but in the same direction) so we travelled together. I loved Ronnie. We were both crazy about quizzes and devised fiendish questions for each other to pass the time. We laughed a lot. He made what could have been dreary train journeys a joy. No one was more thrilled than me when he went on to become a successful actor in the theatre (notable as Smiler in *Chips with Everything*) and in major Hollywood films. He worked with Schwarzenegger and Clint Eastwood, and of course, is remembered for his wonderful turn as the Nazi villain in *Raiders of the Lost Ark*. He died far too young. I'll never forget his friendship, nor the laughter.

I celebrated my 17th birthday at Colchester. There was a pre-Christmas party that evening. A great way to spend my birthday with all these lovely people. William (Bill) Hobbs, who went on to become the top fight director at the National

Theatre and in films, excitedly brought out an LP record he'd just bought of the thrilling new show everyone was talking about. I heard the opening of the record and dismissed it. I couldn't see what the fuss was about. It was *West Side Story*! It happens now to be far and away my favourite musical. My excuse for not 'getting it' then was that I knew nothing of musicals – and, after all, I was only 17!

I went home after my Colchester stint for a post-Christmas break. My mother's friend, Silas Harvey (who was the Drama Advisor for Northumberland) was worried about me just drifting from job to job on my own in London. He suggested I apply to a drama school and get a proper training.

I remember feeling a great sense of relief. I could now spend my time at home until September – if I managed to get into Rose Bruford's, of course. I had wanted to go to RADA (I'd not really heard of the others) but that was out of the question. We couldn't afford it. But the Rose Bruford three-year acting course incorporated a teaching element and after the three years I would come away with a teaching diploma. The Northumberland Education committee would give me a grant for Bruford's. So, Bruford's it had to be. I had to get in. But… because teaching was a vital element of the course, I needed more O-Levels than I had. Would I be able to get them all in time for starting in September? But more importantly, would I get in?

The prospectus was very impressive. Rose Bruford herself was at the helm and it seemed she was a brilliant all-rounder. A verse speaker par excellence, she had published books on speech and drama and teaching mime, she was even accomplished at fencing. The photograph on the front of prospectus showed a handsome building with a grassy lawn surrounded by trees leading down to a lake. Who wouldn't want to study there? It was just outside London, in Kent. Sidcup, to be precise. Not exactly at the throbbing heart of the metropolis.

To get into Rose Bruford's, you had to be 18. I was 17 and I certainly didn't want to hang around for a year waiting for my next birthday. The prospectus also stated that to apply for the course, you needed to have five O-Levels or two A-Levels or equivalent. As I'd left school when I was 16 to go to London and seek my 'fame and fortune', I had only taken a couple of O-levels, reckoning that I wouldn't need them for my career. However, there was a sentence underneath the 'requirements for entry' section that stated that 'in exceptional circumstances' they would take students who weren't 18 or who didn't have the relevant qualifications.

The audition and interviews took almost a whole day and involved writing an essay as well as doing an improvised scene with a couple of others. Within a week of auditioning, I'd received the letter accepting me as a student. The 'exceptional circumstances' that got me in aged-17 and without the required qualifications, were that I'd already had quite a career as a professional actor. To say I was thrilled was an understatement.

Although I'd had a lot of professional experience, I was conscious that I needed help in movement and speech, and a chance to stretch myself as an actor playing parts that I'd not get in the theatre. Being allowed to fail. I was ready, if they were!

Chapter 4

Some weeks before I started at Rose Bruford's, I got a letter from Tom Dickinson. He was already at Bruford's and somehow, he'd found out that I was joining in September. He'd noticed I was from the north-east as was he (a miner's son from Ashington) and he told me that if I'd not yet got fixed up with 'digs' then he recommended I stay with his landlady, Mrs Wareham, 'the best in Sidcup'. It was very sweet of him and I did indeed contact the formidable Mrs W. I stayed with her for my three years at Bruford's and Tom was right. She was a splendid Welsh landlady who not only cooked hearty meals but did our washing and ironing. Wow! I'd landed on my feet, thanks to Tom.

I don't know what it's like now but the first day for 'freshers' was a terrible ordeal. The newcomers had to perform in front of the rest of the college. First, we had to announce ourselves and give a brief résumé of our life thus far, and then recite a poem. Later, in groups of four, we had to perform an improvised scene on a given subject. People who were in the audience told me afterwards that as I walked onstage, they saw a very young-looking, gauche, self-conscious lad with a red cardigan and an orange shirt that clashed terribly. They all said how surprised they were when I started to speak. Out came this unexpectedly baritone voice. The poem I'd chosen was *The Burning of the Leaves* by Laurence Binyon that I'd done in a poetry exam not long before. I later learned it was Rose Bruford's least favourite poem!

The improvised scene was an embarrassing shamble. The whole experience was terrifying. And that was the point, apparently. Miss Bruford reckoned that whatever we chose to do with our lives, whether we chose the stage or the classroom, we'd never have to face an ordeal so frightening. I was expecting the older students in the audience to be critical but a year later, when it was my turn to watch rather than participate, I found that I (and my fellow students) were sympathetic and encouraging and wanting the newcomers to do well.

I had a terrific time at the Rose Bruford Training College of Speech and Drama. I learned so much but initially, I felt a bit out of things. So many of the students there seemed to be 'posh'. I felt a bit of an alien, even though I'd worked in the theatre. I'd led a fairly sheltered life. 'Bru', as everyone (students and staff alike) called Miss Bruford, was, as I mentioned before, an inspiring teacher. I remember one mime class where she got us to mime eating fruit. We'd imagine the feel of, say, the apple in our hand, its shape, its weight. We'd lift it to our mouth ready to eat. We'd smell the tang of it. We'd crunch into it with our teeth. Was it sweet? Tart? Fruity? Floury? We'd chew it and savour the taste. Next, we'd peel and eat an imaginary orange. Then a banana. And then:

"And now, I want you to imagine eating an avocado pear," Bru announced.

A what? I thought, but of course, didn't say. Don't forget this was 1960.

I'd never heard of an avocado pear let alone seen one, so had no idea how to eat one. But… it must be some sort of pear. So I imagined it in my hand and took a big healthy bite out of it. When I asked a friend after the class, he explained to me what an avocado was. I was still none-the-wiser!

Bru was a wonderful verse-speaker. It was a privilege to have classes with her. I have a recording of her on a vinyl LP when she gave a recital at the Royal Festival Hall. It's a masterclass on how to speak verse. Her verse-speaking was economical and subtle. No declaiming, just the words spoken with feeling. I've not heard anyone before or since speak verse better. Wordsworth, TS Eliot or Edith Sitwell, she was perfect in all those styles.

I admired her very much but was terrified of her. We all were. But it's surprising because she was small and not at all aggressive. Never did she raise her voice in anger. She got cross sometimes but her rebuke was always more in sorrow than anger.

Nowadays, Rose Bruford College is like a modern university campus. The beautiful old building that was on the prospectus is seldom used, and there are modern impressive buildings now and a splendid modern theatre. In my day, we had the Barn Theatre which was... well, a barn that had been converted into a theatre with a tiny gallery where Bru and her staff would watch productions.

One of my regrets was that, at Park School, there was no facility for learning a language. They barely taught English! I knew that, at some point in my life, I would use that part of my brain that was crying out to know French or Spanish or Italian. But at Bruford's, we did 'phonetics' which is a sort of language; the language of speech sounds. Using phonetics, I was able to write down how someone spoke. I took to it like a duck takes to water. I was soon able to write the phonetic notation at dictation speed. I'd take notes at lectures using the phonetic symbols. To others, it seemed horribly pretentious; to me, it was the perfect way to practise the symbols. It was through studying phonetics that I was able to 'cure' a pronunciation problem I had: the way I said the word 'one'. I still pronounced it the Geordie way (rhyming with 'gone') and not as I was encouraged to do, to sound more like won (wun). I couldn't hear the difference – until I did phonetics. Seeing the two words written with the phonetic symbols, I could see where I was going wrong and was able to correct it. Now, of course, a Geordie accent is acceptable and even encouraged. But I can't stress enough that then, even the small problem of pronouncing 'one' was regarded as a hindrance and a problem. Our phonetics teacher was Margaret (Greta) Stevens, and like Bru, a fine teacher.

On Saturday morning, selected students would perform for local children in the Barn Theatre. There was little chance for performing in the first year, at least not in front of an audience, so I was thrilled to get the part of Stuffy, a Billy Bunter type character (with padding!) in a musical play called *Where Do We Go from Here?* which was written by another teacher, Helga Burgess, with music by Barbara Lander who accompanied a lot of our movement classes. Helga taught something called 'Greek dancing', for which we had to wear chitons, short shift-like garments. I am afraid we misbehaved during these classes. We couldn't see the point of doing this. When were we ever going to need to do Greek dancing? We were right. The last time I did any ancient Greek dancing was at Bruford's, although I have to say that people still talk today about my Pyrrhic war dance!

Where Do We Go from Here? was a jolly show with some catchy Barbara Lander songs. I was lucky to get a role in it because the cast was made up of the three years, and obviously, where possible, the seniors got priority casting.

Another Saturday morning show was *L'enfant Prodigue* – a three-act mime play with music by André Wormser. This was a show for those who moved well. That didn't include me. It was a charming and touching piece and the music by Wormser was delightful. The show used *Commedia dell'arte* gestures and it was felt that to demonstrate what the gestures meant, a character dressed as Harlequin should come onstage at the beginning and explain to the children what the gestures meant and, generally, give a lively introduction to what they were to see. There was nothing in the script so there was a little competition instigated by Bru for someone to come up with appropriate dialogue. I'd written something, more in the hope of getting the part of Harlequin who didn't have a lot of 'dance' to do. He just needed to be fun and communicate with the audience.

A little while later, I was called to Rose Bruford's office. It was rare to go into that 'holy of holies'. I was terrified rather as I had been at junior school; I feared the worst. I sat in front of Bru's huge desk quaking. She smiled. She had the loveliest smile. Her eyes and her whole face lit up. I had won the competition! They were going to use my script.

"It's perfect. We've hardly changed your script at all."
Then she added the sting in the tail, "And Bernard Holley will
be splendid saying it!"

So, mixed blessings. As I was leaving feeling very good
but a bit disappointed, she called out:

"By the way, it's different 'from', never different 'to', as
you have written. Goodbye."

I have never said 'different to' to this day. I always say
'different from' and even though there are some who say
there's nothing wrong with 'different to', you will never hear
me saying it!

I remember in the *New Statesman* they'd printed an article
about the very posh writer, Marghanita Laski. In the next
edition, they published a letter from her, thanking the NS for
the article. Then came the withering phrase (as she'd
obviously been misquoted) – *But,* she ended, *we never say
different to in Hampstead!*

The three-year course at Bruford's was nothing if not
comprehensive. The idea was that everyone who left college
to go into theatre had a thorough training. Often, in those days,
a first theatre job would mean working in rep as an
acting/ASM (assistant stage manager). Rose Bruford students
were often hired because they'd been thoroughly taught
everything to do with running a show backstage from lighting
to prop-making, from sound to backstage etiquette. The stage-
management teacher was a scary Scots woman called Jonny.
She had a vicious temper and took no prisoners. I knew my
way around backstage but I was pretty useless at making
things but for some reason Jonny liked me and never bawled
me out as she often did the others.

The girls all fancied the handsome, Peter Krumins, who
taught set design, but I don't remember that we even did any
designing.

But we all had fun in Doris Salter's 'costume' class. She
was a sweet-looking old lady with an easy-to-imitate
querulous voice. She gave lectures on the history of costume
and we sometimes had to make simple period clothes. She was
a great fan of using felt to make period clothes. She once

advised us that the 'best place to get felt was Lewisham High Street!'. You can guess how we all burst out in laughter at that comment. She looked so innocent but talking to students who'd been to her classes in previous and, indeed, later years, they were able to come up with the same quote. Dear Miss Salter knew exactly what she was doing throwing in all those 'double entendres'.

We had the choice of taking classes in fencing or singing. It's unbelievable now to think that most of us chose fencing. Singing was of no use to us, we were actors! In those days, there was a huge division between 'legit' acting and musical theatre. I did once take singing for one term and enjoyed singing Italian songs but I kept thinking, *What's the point of this?* and went back to fencing which was going to be much more useful to me!

Because the course involved a teaching element, we had a number of classes on teaching technique and education lectures. It was all a bit turgid and dull for those of us who had no intention of teaching but it had to be done. In our first year, each of us was assigned an infant school in the area. We'd spend a morning there once a week. In the second year, it was a junior school, and in the third, we spent half a day and a week before term started, at a senior school. Of course, the infant school was a doddle. Lovely teachers and attentive and charming children. Inevitably, I was asked to read stories. There is no better audience than children. You'll know when they are bored but when they are engaged, then it's wonderful to see the bright, attentive eyes on you, listening to every word. I enjoyed it as much as they seemed to.

As I mentioned before, English was my subject. I loved words. I understood grammar. I knew what a gerund was and how to use it. But… and it's a big 'but', I was and still am a poor speller (I rely a lot these days on spell-check). I don't know why it should be. I have a logical mind and spelling never seemed to me to be logical. I did try to improve and learn how a word was spelt. That worked to an extent but it didn't come naturally to me. In this particular infant class that I'd been assigned to, the children all had small bright exercise books with *My Spelling Book* written on the front. If they didn't know how to spell a particular word, they could come to the teacher and she would write the word, correctly spelled, for the child. The children were also encouraged to make a drawing beside the word, where possible, to help them remember. Whilst I was sitting in with the class-teacher, she told the children that if they needed to have a word spelled out during the class that they should come to me and I would write it out (in large clear writing) for them in their books. On one occasion, a serious little boy came to me with his book. I asked him what word he wanted me to write for him. I saw that he'd drawn a sailing boat. "Yacht," he told me. I know how to spell it now, of course. But then my mind went blank and I wrote in beautiful big letters 'yaught'. Even as I recall this episode now, I shudder and feel the embarrassment. Particularly as I had to dash to my dictionary later to check what I suspected was the wrong spelling. It was, of course. Mortification!

In my second year, I taught juniors. It was another friendly school, but I was asked if I'd take History with one particular class. I was supposed to be teaching drama but I agreed to help out. I just read about the subject and chatted to the kids about it. I did teach some drama, but mostly, I was teaching English and the Tudors!

After I had taken the final lesson, the teacher asked me to wait behind for a couple of minutes. A rather shy boy came forward with an enormous card and a beautifully wrapped package. The jolly card said *"thank you for being such a very nice teacher"* and wishing me luck for the future. I unwrapped the parcel and there was a pretty mug filled with an assortment of sweets. In a much smaller package was a collection of penny, halfpenny and threepenny bit coins. The teacher explained that the children had got together and put money towards the present and card for me. There was some change left over hence the smaller package. She assured me that the children did it off their own bat, she had nothing to do with it. I was so moved I could hardly speak. I thanked them so much. I was afraid of saying too much more. I was on the verge of bursting into tears!

My third-year stint was at an all boys' school in Orpington. I was by then 19 but looked younger than a lot of the boys I was teaching. Teaching? I was supposed to teach them English and drama but because the hall was being used for other classes, I had to teach drama in the classroom. I'd worked out various scenarios without having to move the desks around too much. These lads recognised that they had an easy target. They were not going to do drama! One of the 'fail-safe' techniques we were taught in 'teaching method' lessons was that when a class was unruly, one should just stand there, saying nothing. Eventually, the pupils would get curious, and slowly but surely, they'd stop their row and then the teacher could get on with the lesson. I am here to tell you that this method does not work! Or, at least, it didn't work for me. The noise got worse. I was despairing. I just didn't know what to do. I pleaded. I cajoled, I raged, I negotiated. All to no avail. Eventually, a teacher from the next class burst in. Before he'd even said anything, the class shut up instantly. I stood there pathetically grateful but very embarrassed especially when he said, "Mr Griffin is a guest in our school. What is he going to think of your behaviour? You are putting our school to shame. If I hear one more peep out of you, there will be serious trouble." Not my finest moment! They were reasonably well behaved for the rest of the class. But they had won.

My experiences as a teacher, therefore, were mixed. I didn't mind. I remember the huge relief I felt the day I left that Orpington school for the last time. I was never going to be a teacher. I was going to be an actor. I would make sure I got the teaching qualification. But I would also make sure that I'd never ever have to use it.

Chapter 5

So, the training at Bruford's was comprehensive. In one area, they were ahead of other schools. At the top of the old building, near the staff room and costume workshops, a couple of rooms had been converted into a radio studio. 'Radio technique' was on the timetable and students received a rudimentary training in the skills of broadcasting. Each year, there was a competition at the BBC open to all drama schools. The students would read scenes from a couple of plays and a short solo piece. Because the college had a studio, Bruford students had an advantage. The top prize was a contract with the BBC Drama Repertory Company, in those days a wonderful group of actors who were contracted to appear in radio plays, or indeed, in any radio programme that required a 'voice'. It was a year's contract. A wonderful opportunity for a young actor (I use 'actor' here for male or female) and Bruford students invariably won.

The pieces that were chosen for me when I was entered in my final year were not particularly useful, but I felt I'd done well enough to make the judges take notice. I didn't win but hoped perhaps I'd made an impression. I was commended and the whole experience gave me confidence for when I did take the BBC radio general audition a few years later. This time I passed.

I enjoyed my time at Bruford's. I learned a lot and got to play a wide variety of roles. More children's theatre, my first Shakespearean parts and I was a lively and energetic Tony Lumpkin in *She Stoops to Conquer*. But in my final year I was picked to play Billy Liar. Wow! It had not long been in the West End starring Albert Finney and now I was going to have a shot at it. I was so excited that I couldn't sleep. This was it.

This was my moment to show everyone what I could do. My moment to shine. There is a moment when Billy is onstage by himself. The script gives him various things to do. How they are done depends on the actor playing the part. The director, Douglas Storm, allowed me to work out a routine for myself. It was an interesting experiment for me because I knew instinctively what to do and how to do it and what would work and what wouldn't.

I was very nervous to be playing such a huge role, but I remember thinking before the curtain went up on the first performance, *No time for nerves. This is the moment you have been waiting for. OK, do it!* It was one of the best performances I have ever given. It was such a wonderful part and I understood Billy so well. I nailed it. This is not boasting, just a fact. Many times, I certainly did not come to grips with a part. If I'd failed as Billy, it would have been very disappointing but acceptable. This is what drama school training is for – trying to succeed but having the courage to fail. I succeeded with Billy. The roar at the end was something I can still hear. It seemed as though half the audience came to my dressing room afterwards. I was ridiculously happy. I'd taken on a big challenge and I'd made a success of it. I was an actor.

The third year dragged a bit. I had learned a lot at Bru's but I now wanted to put what I'd learned into practice. I was eager to get going.

At the end of every year, Rose Bruford mounted The Big Show. This show was presented in the final week of the final term each year and the entire college was involved. If you weren't in it, then you were assigned to a department: costume, props, publicity, stage-management etc. I was in all the shows although had small parts in my first year in a gloomy religious piece called *The Dark Hours* which told of the last days of Christ. I don't remember much about it except that we laughed a lot. The dialogue was pretty awful (despite being written by Don Marquis of *archy and mehitabel* fame).

In my second year the chosen show was *Cyrano de Bergerac* with two very fine actors playing Cyrano and

Christian. Charles Thomas was the student we all thought was going to be a big star. He had it all: charisma, looks and great acting skills. His Cyrano was dazzling. Charlie soon went off to the RSC and was playing very good roles there, including Orsino. It was during a tour of Australia with the RSC that he was found dead in his hotel room of a drug overdose. There is no doubt he would have become as successful as his contemporary, Ian McKellen. Malcolm Tierney did very well as Christian although he would have been the first to admit he wasn't the moony romantic type. Malcolm too had a successful career although I think it was hampered by his extreme left political views. Not that I objected to that but I know it put off some managements. They didn't want an agitator from the Worker's Revolutionary Party in their companies. Pity.

The third year was our big show. The show was presented on a large scale at a major theatre in London. Ours was to be performed at Sadler's Wells. Don't forget this was our showpiece. This was the show in which we hoped we would be spotted by agents or producers and whisked off to be stars. The show chosen for our big show was *Green Pastures* by Marc Connelly. For those of you who don't know it, *Green Pastures* is a musical play of stories from the Bible – performed by black people! This was 1963 and I am ashamed to say that we all 'blacked up' for it. But that wasn't our objection then. It was: 'How are agents and producers going to know who is who if we are all covered in black makeup?'

The spirituals were fun to sing but when I look at the photograph of Noah and his three sons from our production, I can barely recognise myself as Shem. If I can't recognise myself, then how would an agent! Of course, they were given 10x8 photos of us as we really were, but we were not very happy. Actually, I was offered a job after the final performance! A year's tour (mostly in Scotland) with a children's theatre company. My instinct has always been good. Even when I was pressurised by my elocution teacher to accept the part of the boy king in the amateur production *The Sleeping Prince*, I knew that I wanted to do the play with

Tynemouth Repertory Theatre and not just because I got paid for it. My instinct said, *take the rep job,* and, of course, it was the right decision. I knew I didn't want to accept the children's theatre job even though it meant turning down a year's work. Again, as you'll see, it was the right choice.

This was a time of big changes. We felt it. We were all excited when one of our colleagues was arrested in London on a Ban the Bomb march. There was a feeling of protest in the air. The young people wanted a different world. It manifested itself at Bruford's during my third year.

We'd often have story-telling or verse-speaking competitions. For one memorable Chaucer festival, I was handed a prize from the great John Masefield. It seemed so odd that a poet I'd studied at school and who I'd imagined was long dead, should be shaking my hand.

There was a sonnet competition for the second and third years to be judged by a formidable actress friend of Bru's. We all had to learn a sonnet and present it to the audience of students and staff. We had to have a second one prepared too, in case the 'judge' wanted to hear another one. No one was asked to perform the second one until Liz. The elderly actress asked to hear Liz's second choice. Like all of us, Liz had one ready but hadn't learnt it which annoyed the 'judge' (who I will call Miss Dour) very much. She was very rude to Liz who took it in her stride but the audience was getting restless and there was a definite feeling of animosity towards Miss Dour.

At the end of the performance, Miss Dour came onto the stage to give her verdict. She was imperious and haughty. Keith, a fellow student (who was in the wings stage-managing the event) was instructed to record Miss Dour's words of wisdom so he pressed the 'play' button of the tape-machine. Miss Dour began her pronouncements. She'd only been talking a few minutes when she glanced into the wings and saw Keith and his tape-machine. She raged at him. "How dare you record me without my permission?" She may very well have had a point but her rudeness was unacceptable and Keith was only doing what he'd been asked to. It was not his fault. Slowly but steadily the students in the audience started a slow handclap. They'd had enough of Miss Dour's high-handedness. The clapping got louder, booing was heard. Miss Bruford tore through the audience and leapt onto the stage beside a now seething Miss Dour.

"Stop this noise at once! At once, do you hear?" Miss Bruford yelled over the increasing din. The slow handclaps were now accompanied by stamping feet. The students wouldn't stop. It was an electrifying moment. It was much more than a student protest at a very rude old actress. It felt as though this was a seismic shift in how things were going to be in the future. The youth would have their say, their voices would be heard.

It was the only time I saw Rose Bruford really angry. If she had been critical of anyone or any group of students, her attitude was one of disappointment. She almost never raised her voice. She was generally reasonable and kindly. So why were we all so in awe of her? Why did we quake when we saw her coming down the corridor towards us? She was physically very small and she had a pleasant and friendly face. But there is no question that most of us were wary of her. I suppose it was because she was 'the boss'. She could 'hire and fire'. And, of course, she was Rose Bruford. Not just a marvellous and inspiring teacher but the Principal (with a capital P).

But I was thrilled, years later, to get to know her much better as a warm and friendly person, sweet and shy and (yes, really!) vulnerable.

It was around 1970 and I was performing at the famous Players Theatre. The Players was a long-established music hall company that performed authentic music hall songs to enthusiastic audiences. It was a wonderful institution where many famous performers had appeared including Peter Ustinov, Maggie Smith and Hattie Jacques. I was lucky enough to perform there with some of the 'old-timers' like the indefatigable Joan Sterndale Bennett and the amazing Archie Harradine. When I worked there, Archie was pretty old. He had a very bad stammer offstage but onstage, not only did the stammer disappear, but he specialised in very fast patter songs. I was still pretty boyish and performed either 'saucy sailor' numbers or as lovelorn young men who were put upon by women. It was a lot of fun.

Not content with running her college during term time, Rose Bruford often ran summer courses at the college for American students. Unbeknownst to me, she often took her students to the Players Theatre to see shows that were uniquely and quintessentially English.

One evening, after I had been performing, I went into the Players' Bar to have a drink before heading home and there she was: Bru, surrounded by her students. How different the situation was! I was full of confidence and Bru was rather shy but proudly introduced me to her students. The Players was a club and I asked if she was a member. She told me she wasn't but was on the waiting list. I went straight to the box office and the wonderful Cynthia who ran the front of house. After a few minutes of explanation to Cynthia, I was thrilled to be able to go back into the bar with Rose Bruford's Players' membership card!

I coincided with her once more during that summer at the Players. She insisted I keep in touch with her. I felt I was fairly anonymous while at Bruford's so I was surprised that Rose seemed to know all that I'd been doing since I'd left in 1963.

Eventually, inevitably, Rose Bruford retired and went to live near Dartford. She gave me her address. The college doctor was Dr Marie (I don't think any of us knew her surname and I had no call to visit her surgery during my time at college). What I didn't know then was that Bru and Dr Marie were devoted friends. When I'd heard that Dr Marie had died, I wrote to Bru saying how sad I was to hear the news. The letter I received from Rose, in her very distinctive handwriting, was so moving, so touching and so personal. She described how desolate life without Marie was, how she was finding it very difficult to come to terms with the death of her friend. She asked me to contact Jimmy (an ex-student who had been a teacher at the college when I was there) and get him to drive me to Dartford to see her. I phoned him three times and left messages. I don't drive, so to go to Dartford with Jimmy would've been perfect. He didn't reply to my answer-machine messages. I was about to try one more time when I received the news that Rose had died. I was frustrated and a bit angry that I'd not tried even harder. But I still have that last letter she wrote to me. Rose Bruford, a remarkable woman.

Rose Bruford College is like a university campus now with a state-of-the-art theatre. The lovely old building, which is where most of our classes took place, is hardly used. As you go into the busy reception area there is a painting of Bru. At one time, it would have struck fear into me. Now I smile.

Chapter 6

Towards the end of term, there were regular meetings with Rose Bruford and the third-year students. Miss Bruford would read out a list of jobs that had come in – for teachers – and encouraged us to apply for them. Many did, in fact most of our year went on to have careers in education.

We were a rebellious year and of the thirty-plus students who started in the first year, we ended up with only nineteen. Some were kicked out, some didn't want to stay, a couple of girls got pregnant... Very few of those who were left went into acting. I was one of six or seven. And I am still here!

I remember talking to Bernie, the guy I shared my digs with in my final year, not long before we left college. What were our ambitions? His were clear-cut. He wanted to be at the RSC before he was thirty and to be playing a good part in a TV series by the age of 40. My ambitions were not so specific. I remember saying that I just wanted to work. I wanted to make my living as an actor. Bernie did well and did indeed play a leading part in a TV series although he didn't get into the RSC. And I succeeded in my ambition too. I did make my living as an actor.

One of the final shows we did in that last year was the end-of-term revue. This was where those of us who were leaving, could perform sketches and songs taking a satirical and often nostalgic look at our three years at the college. My friend, Jenny Berg and I wrote most of it. In my final year I played the main character in the Saturday Children's Theatre show called *The Treasure of Castle Blount*. In the show, I came on at the beginning singing, *I've lost my way in the big wide world and it's going to take some finding*. The Barn theatre stage had a trapdoor and, in the revue, I came on in my costume singing the song: *I've lost my way in the big waaaaaaaaaaaah!* I fell down through the open trapdoor onto a couple of mattresses under the stage. It got a huge laugh and I didn't break any bones!

There was a spoof of *This is Your Life* and even a sketch with the *Steptoe and Son* characters (that dates it!) and there wasn't a dry eye in the house when, at the end of the show, the entire cast stood on the stage and sang *The Course is Over* (to the tune of The Jule Styne/Comden and Green song, *The Party's Over*).

The course is over
It's time to call it a day
It's time to turn off the lights and pack dusty tights
Away...
The course is over
We've loved it being with you
We've had a wonderful time improving our mime
With Greta and Bru...

You get the picture.

I realised that I had a reputation for writing satirical songs when many years later at a reunion, a fellow student asked if I was still writing songs. The answer was that I wasn't really, except for the special verses for friend's birthdays and so on. But it was a surprise that that's what I was remembered for.

The big day came when we received our RBTC diplomas from the actress Barbara Jefford. I knew that I had no intention of using the teaching diploma so the actual document wasn't worth much except that it showed us all that we had done it (three of our year 'failed' and suddenly they weren't there anymore which was horrible) and we'd achieved our goals. I got special commendation on my diploma for phonetics, mime and (interestingly, given where I ended up) storytelling. I only failed one subject: makeup! This has always seemed to me rather silly. How do you fail makeup? In the unlikely event I were to play Fagin or Long John Silver then I'd practise, consult, experiment until I got the makeup right. At Bruford's,

Leo Baker, who was in charge of the makeup class, would say something like: "Alright, class. Gentlemen, you have one hour to make yourselves up as either a Regency fob, a Pirate King or Shylock. Ready. Go!" It was ridiculous. I couldn't do it. I deserved to fail. Although I have to say that I never ever have had any problems with makeup in my very long career. Failing makeup didn't affect my career! It wasn't really a requirement on radio!

My parents came to collect me and my stuff from my digs, and we all spent a few days in London together. My dad never took holidays so this was a rare time for the three of us to be together. For the first time, before or since, the three of us went to the theatre. We saw Tommy Steele in *Half a Sixpence*. My mother loved it. She was completely taken in by Steele's (I thought) overdone 'charm'. My dad and I both preferred the spectacular *Blitz*! It really was spectacular. The actual blitz sequence, when it seemed half the set was collapsing to the ground accompanied by the deafening noises of bombs and collapsing buildings, was thrilling. The show also happens to contain some of Lionel Bart's best songs. Clever and very much in period.

I went back home for a few days and then, having nowhere to stay in London, I joined three actresses from my year who'd decided to stay on in Sidcup. There, we wrote hundreds of work letters. And waited for the first job to come along.

The flat was lovely, spacious, airy and sunny. We ate wonderfully healthy food but we had to be frugal and our trips to the local cinema had to be rationed. We shared the house with some mice which wasn't pleasant. I discovered later that I was musophobic. I did have an irrational fear or mice and rats. Luckily, in my long life, I have not met many.

I mentioned earlier that Tom Dickinson, a fellow Geordie, had contacted me before I went to Bru's to recommend I stay in his 'digs' – 'the best in Sidcup'. I did stay there and he was right. They were the best. Now Tom came up trumps again. He'd left Bruford's a year ahead of me and was currently working in rep at Lincoln. They were going to be doing a production of the play, *French for Love*, and there was 'a perfect part for you' he told me. He'd mentioned me to Kay Gardner who was running the theatre and hey presto! I got the part without even having to audition. My first role after leaving Rose Bruford's.

French for Love was a play about the 'rites of passage' of a self-conscious teenager on holiday in rural France who is seduced by an attractive older French woman. I haven't been able to track down the play but it was a popular play with reps in its day. I noticed with a kind of horror, that the agent who had chased me around his flat, had played my part when it was first done in the West End years before.

I said my goodbyes to the 'girls' at a wonderful farewell meal they made and on Sunday headed off to Lincoln. Tom had said that digs were hard to find but he sent me a list. I found myself a place not far from the theatre. It wasn't ideal. It was at the top of a steep hill on the right of which was the stunningly impressive Cathedral. I discovered that I was sharing my room with three others, all construction workers who were up and breakfasted before I'd even stirred. But that didn't matter at all. I had a lovely part and as I set off for my first rehearsal, there was a definite spring in my step.

At that time, Lincoln rep had a couple of companies on the go. One would be playing in the main house in Lincoln and the other would do a mini-tour to the theatre at Rotherham or Loughborough. We were to open at the Civic Theatre in Rotherham, a converted church. All I remember about it was that you couldn't go to the loo during a performance. Well, you could, but you couldn't use the flush as the noise could be heard onstage.

I don't remember much about the play or the production except that the cast was friendly and I was in seventh heaven.

It was while I was at Rotherham that I filled in the Equity forms to become a member of our union. The proposer was our director, Salvin Stewart. Salvin was a larger than life character (in all senses) and he was later to gather a bunch of fans for his performance in an early series of *Dr Who*. One evening, before the show, he came into my dressing room to give me some notes. He'd been in to see the show the previous evening. As he was leaving, almost casually, he said, "Oh, by the way, Geoffrey Ost was in to see the show last night. He thought you were excellent!"

Wow! Geoffrey Ost ran the Playhouse Theatre in Sheffield, one of the leading repertory theatres at the time. Most actors leaving drama school knew in those days that, to get experience, they could go into rep. Most towns and cities had their local rep companies. Some, like Tynemouth where I made my professional debut aged-13, were 'weekly' reps.

Weekly rep was tough: whilst play A was being performed in the evening, play B was being rehearsed during the day. When play A ended its weekly run, play B opened. After the first night of play B, play C went into rehearsal. It's amazing that actors could get together a performance in so short a time, let alone learn the words and yet I saw many excellent performances in weekly rep. Fortnightly reps (like Lincoln) were less frenetic and frantic but we drama students dreamed of getting into a three-weekly rep like Bristol or Birmingham… or Sheffield.

Geoffrey Ost was a legend. He'd started the Sheffield Repertory Theatre in 1936 and gave many young actors their early chances to shine (Nigel Hawthorne, Patrick McGoohan, Keith Barron and Peter Sallis – to name but a few). He was very much of the 'old school': charming, a gentleman with impeccable manners. To work for him at Sheffield would be amazing.

I found the telephone number for the Playhouse, and the next morning, I plucked up courage and dialled. Good fortune was on my side. Geoffrey picked up the phone. I nervously gabbled, "Oh, Mr Ost, my name's Gordon Griffin. I understand you liked my performance last night in *French for Love* and I just wondered that if you were casting any parts that you thought I'd be suitable for you'd consider me."

There was a pause, and then came this lovely, warm, relaxed voice, "Actually, there is a part I am casting that you could play for us. Clarence Day Jr in the American comedy, *Life with Father*…"

And that was it. No interview. No audition. I'd not even been asked if I could do an American accent. I was sent a contract. I was to play a very good part in what was then the longest running play that Broadway had ever known. I was going to Sheffield. And I had not been there before. I had not even met Geoffrey Ost.

Life with Father! Life was good!

Chapter 7

Sheffield. Wonderful part. Excellent company. Great experience. But I nearly got off on the wrong footing. I arrived in Sheffield for the first time the day before I was to start rehearsals. I had the addresses of three potential 'digs' so I set off to visit them all. One was miles away and involved two bus rides and this in a city I didn't know. Not one of the places I visited had any vacancies. It was getting dark and I was cold. I went back to the theatre to search out the stage manager to see what she suggested I do. Enter Madge D'Alroy, the wardrobe mistress. Maternal, warm, sweet-natured Madge. She'd heard of my plight and told me that she had a small ("very small", she emphasised) room in her house if I was really desperate. I was really desperate. The room was indeed small. But it was cosy and warm. It was to be my home for the next fifteen months.

Before heading back to Madge's house, I checked my call for the next day. The call-sheet was rather complicated but I saw that my character was required at 10:30. So not a horribly early start.

I was sharing my digs with another member of the company, Angela Thorne. She was delightful and, as she'd been with the company for a few months, she was able to give me advice. She was warm and welcoming.

Rehearsals were to take place on the stage. The set of the current production had been cleared out of the way. Tapes on the stage marked the outline of the *Life with Father* set. I nervously stepped onto the stage about ten minutes before my allotted time of 10:30. Everyone stared at me. Colin George, the director, didn't look happy.

"Where have you been? We have been waiting for you. We couldn't start until you got here."

I'd not met Colin before and I must say I was disappointed with this welcome. After all, I was early, not late. Except that I *was* late. I had misread the call-sheet. All the cast was called at ten. Far from being ten minutes early, I was twenty minutes late. I have always been pathologically punctual to the point where I will often arrive for appointments (especially at places I had not been to before) far too early. So, to be late in any case was shocking to me. To be late for my first day of rehearsal on such an important day made me feel physically sick. Gradually, everyone relaxed and we got down the rehearsals. The actors were understanding and kind. The first reading went well. Only Colin remained grumpy and curt. I didn't really blame him. It was a wretched start to my first day.

The embarrassment of the first rehearsal soon disappeared. Everyone was friendly, rehearsals went well.

Clarence Day Jr was a real person; *Life with Father* was his memoir of growing up in a well-to-do household with a domineering father. The stories were turned into a hugely successful Broadway play by Russel Crouse and Howard Lindsay who later wrote the book for Rodgers and Hammerstein's *The Sound of Music*.

There were four Day children in the play, in real life they were all redheads and I am not sure who at the theatre thought it would be good publicity if Chris Wilkinson (who played Clarence's slightly younger brother) and myself had our hair dyed bright red. But we duly arrived at a hairdresser near the theatre, where, before our very eyes, we became carrot-tops. The press was indeed there and we did get quite a lot of publicity. It meant I was redheaded for quite a while until my naturally fair hair grew back again. The two younger children were at school so had red wigs, as did Elspeth McNaughton and James Locker who played my parents.

Clarence Day Jr was a lovely part to play and I was surrounded by a splendid cast and a superb set. My 'love interest' in the play was provided by a delightful young actress, Vickery Turner. Vickery went on to great things, winning a batch of awards playing opposite Vanessa Redgrave in the stage version of *The Prime of Miss Jean Brodie*. Not content with being a successful stage, television and film actress, she also wrote novels and plays, and at one point was married to the Hollywood actor, Warren Oates. She died tragically young. We got on famously. I enjoyed my scenes with her very much.

The reviews for the play and for me were very good, so much so that I was asked to join the company. I still recall squealing with sheer joy at the news especially as I was next cast in another leading part in a four-handed comedy called *Foursome Reel*.

The company at the Playhouse was a strong one. The leading lady was Anne Stallybrass who played many a gritty northern lass on television but is probably best remembered for playing one of the leading characters in *The Onedin Line*. Anne was a strong lady who didn't suffer fools but I liked her enormously and she was very kind to me and put in the odd good word for me with television producers after I had left.

Later in the season, Anne was cast as Cleopatra in Shakespeare's play. This was not obvious casting but she was mesmerising. The other actors in the play would crowd into the wings to watch her. She was not tall but she towered as Cleopatra. Her then husband, Roger Rowland, was her Antony.

The most impressive performer during my time at Sheffield was Angela Thorne. She got rather typecast on television later as upper-class eccentrics and she did have a 'posh' voice but at Sheffield, she played everything; one minute she was a delightful Berinthia in Vanbrugh's *The Relapse*, then without seeming to bat an eyelid, she was the dumbest of dumb blondes in the Judy Holliday part in *Born Yesterday*. And she was such fun.

Madge, our landlady, gave wonderful parties. I remember one where Angela let her hair down and sang, at the top of her voice, the Petula Clark hit, *Downtown* while dancing around the room like a mad thing. Her chap (she wasn't married to him yet) was Peter Penry-Jones and he joined the company to play, amongst other things, Captain Cat in *Under Milk Wood* in which I gave my Nogood Boyo. When they left Sheffield, Angela and Peter married, and are the parents of two strapping actors, Rupert and Toby Penry-Jones.

Talking of *Under Milk Wood* made me realise what a wonderful training such a rep was for a young actor. You got to play all sorts of parts in all sorts of styles. I did Restoration comedy, Feydeau farce, (*Hotel Paradiso*), Shaw and Shakespeare as well as modern writers like John Whiting and Stan Barstow. When the cast-list went up for, say, *Under Milk Wood*, we didn't say "Oh, I am not sure I can do that" or "I can't do a Welsh accent." You did it. You accepted the challenge. In a company, you'd be expected to play whatever part you were cast in. Sometimes it meant playing characters older than you were, as in *The Masters*, Ronald Millar's stage adaptation of CP Snow's fine novel. It's set in a Cambridge college and has a large cast of dons. It meant that we younger actors had to try to look middle-aged. I had to whiten my 'red' hair and move in a slower and more sedate manner. When I saw that I was to play Lewis Eliot, I straightaway thought about how to play him, a man at least thirty years older than I was. I didn't ever think, *That's impossible. I can't do that*.

Years later, I realised too that working in rep is not unlike recording audiobooks. You can't get fazed by the challenges of characters or accents. You accept the book, you work out how the characters will sound, you prepare, you research, you rehearse and you record. The process is very similar.

In *The Masters*, the splendid Dennis Edwards was playing the leading character of Jago. It was the first night. The scene, the senior common room in an unnamed Cambridge college, was splendidly designed. Most of us were onstage. I (as Lewis Eliot) was playing chess with a colleague, played by Christopher Wilkinson. Suddenly, the splendid chandelier that hung above us came crashing onto the chess table between us, cutting Chris on the hand and face. He did the sensible thing and went offstage to get attended to. I sat there staring at all the broken pieces of glass surrounding me. But Dennis Edwards, who was mid-speech when the crash happened, carried on without batting an eyelid. He crunched over the now-shattered chandelier, picked it up by the wire and, still talking, placed it at the back of the stage out of the way. I think that the curtain eventually came down whilst the stage management swept up the shattered pieces from the stage, and Chris valiantly returned covered in bandages and Elastoplast. But I am sure, Dennis would have carried on regardless and the show would have gone on, uninterrupted.

My time at Sheffield was wonderful and Madge was a wonderful landlady. She'd been in Variety with her husband, Alf, who had been a magician and ventriloquist. He'd retired to help her run her 'digs' except that he was always performing. Sitting down to breakfast, he'd invariably produce a boiled egg from behind my ear which was funny the first time but wore a bit thin eventually. His patter was continual. His whole life seemed to be a performance.

Towards the end of my time at the Playhouse I got a call from Birmingham to go and read for a new TV series. As I was soon to be leaving the Playhouse Company, I asked for permission to go to the interview. I wasn't rehearsing during the day but I was performing in the evening and, at first, the director wasn't keen for me to go. I mightn't get back for the evening performance. I assured him that I'd get the first train out of Sheffield and make sure my audition was before lunch. With that guarantee, I was given permission to go. I did indeed get one of the first trains out of Sheffield. It was a very early start.

I got to the television studios in good time and was given a scene to look at. It was a scene between my character and another. All I had to do was read in my lines. I was ushered in to a large room and, there, behind a long table, sat a formidable group of people: the producer, director, casting director, writer etc. I sat nervously in front of them. I did wonder whether they'd realised that I'd got up really early to get there for the reading. And if they did know, would it influence them in my favour.

The casting director turned to me and said, "Would you like a cup of tea?"

Ah, they did know I'd travelled from Sheffield. They had realised that I had got up at the crack of dawn to be there. I smiled gratefully and said, "Thank you. I'd love a cup of tea."

They all looked at me in a rather perplexed way, I thought. Maybe they hadn't heard me. "Yes, I'd love a cup of tea," I repeated.

Silence. Maybe they weren't talking to me but to someone else in the room. I turned around. No, there was no one else there. To fill the embarrassing silence, I said for a third time, "Yes, thank you. A cup of tea would be very nice."

And then, very slowly, it dawned on me. "Would you like a cup of tea?" was the first line of the scene! It was my cue!

I went bright red. I was so embarrassed. Somehow, I got to the end of the scene and stumbled out and back to Sheffield.

I didn't get the job. That's why I was never in *Crossroads*!

The BBC in Manchester decided that it might be interesting to follow a production at the Playhouse from rehearsal to performance. The play chosen was the Feydeau farce *Hotel Paradiso,* in which I played Georges, a sort of pageboy at the hotel. I was delighted. This would be my first television appearance. There'd be interviews with the actors and scenes shot in the dressing rooms and there'd be some scenes filmed during a performance. One of my best scenes was to be included. All very exciting but then Winston Churchill died. His massive state funeral was going to involve practically every TV camera and cameraman that was available. The documentary was shelved. The world never did get to see my 'Georges'!

I was definitely one of 'Geoffrey Ost's boys'. He'd hired me and cast me in *Life with Father* even though Colin George, Geoffrey's associate, was directing it.

Halfway through the season it was announced that Geoffrey was to be replaced by Colin. Geoffrey was at last leaving the company he had formed and developed. I thought it was very sad. It's true that a new director was probably needed. A new theatre was being built (The Crucible) and it was felt that a more modern director was required. Geoffrey was of the old school. But it seemed his dismissal was handled badly.

There was no real celebration. No chance for those whose careers he'd furthered to say goodbye and thanks to him.

Geoffrey did few productions during my time there. He was 'winding down'. And during the new regime, spearheaded by Colin, my parts were getting smaller. But one production was coming up (*The Tempest*) where I'd show him what I could do. I was the only one in the company who was right to play Ferdinand and I relished the challenge. But, to the surprise and shock of the whole company, especially me, Colin decided to bring in an actor to play Ferdinand. To say I was disappointed is an understatement. I was humiliated. But I got the message. My services were no longer required. The actor, who came up from London to play Ferdinand, had a beautiful costume designed for him. It was magnificent. I (playing the small role of Francisco) had a hired costume. At the costume parade, the actor who was playing Ferdinand looked ludicrous in the designer costume. He looked a mess. It was decided I should swap my costume for his. I'd wear his. I was mortified. I went back to my dressing room and with a belt I'd grabbed from the wardrobe department, I made the costume look great. 'Ferdinand' looked a mess in the hired costume. So it wasn't the costume at fault.

It doesn't give me any pleasure to tell you that the actor playing Ferdinand was dreadful. What am I saying? Of course, it does!

But, as I said, I got the message and went to see Colin. He made no objection when I said I wanted to leave. In fact, he said he felt it was time I moved on into 'new spheres'. I wasn't sure what they would be. But much as though I loved my 15 months at Sheffield, I knew it was time for new challenges.

After *The Tempest*, I headed back to London. My 'revels now' really were 'ended'.

Chapter 8

I had nowhere to stay in London so I camped out on the sitting room floor of Jenny's flat off the Euston Road. I'd only been in London a few days when I received a phone call from my agent. I had an interview at Pinewood studios with the director Stanley Donen. Stanley Donen? 'The' Stanley Donen? The guy who had directed the film, *Seven Brides for Seven Brothers,* and who was behind the camera for one of the most iconic scenes in all films: Gene Kelly 'singing in the rain'. In 1997, he received a Lifetime Achievement Academy Award. But when I met him, he had just directed *Charade* with Audrey Hepburn and Cary Grant. It was set in Paris and had been a big success. It was decided to capitalise on this success and try something similar. This time, the location was London, and the two big stars were Gregory Peck and Sophia Loren.

When you arrive at Pinewood, you're greeted by a rather grand looking half-timbered house. It's behind this house that the massive sound stages are where, in later years, *Star Wars* and a host of *James Bond* films were shot. I arrived at the reception that was in the house. The walls were panelled wood and the interior was very impressive. I told the reception who I was and that I had come to meet Mr Donen. I was asked to wait and I made myself as comfortable as I could on the splendid brown leather sofa. I was, of course, very nervous. Don't forget that at this point in my career, I'd only done theatre and here I was being interview for a major movie.

Eventually, a very well-dressed man came walking slowly but confidently down a very long corridor towards the reception area. As I was the only one waiting, he came over to me, bent down and said rather grandly, "Have you come to see Mr Donen?" I said that I had.

He stood up and strolled back down the corridor. Half way down, he turned around and, rather irritated, indicated that I should follow him. Well, he hadn't said I had to go with him!

In a sort of conference room sat the great man. I sat beside him. He asked what I'd been doing and how old I was and he told me the part he was casting was Fanshawe, an Oxford University student who has a scene with Gregory Peck early in the film and a scene at the end of the picture with both Peck and Sophia Loren. And that was it. I didn't embarrass myself but I knew that, when a film is being cast, you are either right for the part or you're not.

The next day my agent rather casually said, "Oh, by the way, they want you to do *Arabesque*."

I'd only just left Sheffield Playhouse and now I was going to be eyeball to eyeball with Gregory Peck and Sophia Loren. One of the first things I did was write to my friends in Sheffield and very sweetly my letter was pinned on the noticeboard. Everyone, including Colin George, could see that he was right. I had moved into a 'different sphere'.

In *Arabesque*, Peck plays a visiting professor, a hieroglyphics expert. Early in the film, he is lecturing a bunch of students when he notices that one of them, Fanshawe, is fast asleep. He stops his lecture and yells, "Sex," which wakes up young Fanshawe with a start. Not very auspicious but it was to be the first time I was to be seen on any screen. I was so nervous and felt physically sick. As they were doing the final set up for the shot, I found one of the assistant directors and said I needed to go to the loo.

"Well, hurry up. We are just about to shoot."

I dashed to the loo just in time to be violently sick. I quickly washed my hands, wiped my face and dashed back to the set. A few minutes later, I was filming.

Jack Merivale was also in the scene. He was one of the stars of the movie. I don't know whether he knew that I wasn't well, I certainly hadn't said so to anyone. But he offered me a lift home in his chauffeur-driven car. It was such a sweet thing to do. He was living at the time with Vivien Leigh and I know that he was having a tough time with her because she was so ill and fragile. He was a lovely kind man.

It was a long wait before I did my final sequence on the film. I foolishly didn't take any work. I needed to be free for the filming, although no one knew when that was going to be. The scene, which is the final sequence in the film, was one of the last sequences to be shot.

Eventually, I received the call.

In the film, Peck and Loren have lots of adventures: chases, crashed helicopters, hazards galore. But now, all is calm. Pollock and Yasmin (the characters the stars played) are now relaxing in a punt drifting down a rural part of the River Thames. It's all very romantic. Onto the scene comes Fanshawe rowing erratically and not looking where he's going. He crashes into Peck's punt and yells at him. Then he recognises his professor and apologises profusely. Peck says wryly, "I thought it might be you, Fanshawe." With his punt pole he then tries to push my rowing boat from his punt and ends up sliding down his pole into the water. He pretends to the Sophia Loren character (Yasmin) that he can't swim. She panics and jumps into the water to rescue him. They have some banter, laugh and kiss as Fanshawe rows away. End of film.

In the movie that sequence lasts no more than a couple of minutes but it took three whole days to film. It was fairly complicated. Peck sliding down the punt pole into the water didn't quite satisfy Donen, so it was done again. And again. And again. Every time, the uncomplaining actor had to go back to his caravan, dry off and come back in the same clothes to match up the shot.

Eventually, after many takes, Donen was satisfied. Then came the shot where Sophia Loren (holding her noise) jumps into the water. I can vouch for the fact that the water was freezing cold. But what a trouper she was. She leapt in and did the sequence without a hitch.

I'd love to be able to say that Sophia Loren became my new best friend but I didn't get to know her at all, of course. I was playing a very small part and she was every inch the star, although the crew really took to her – always a good sign. They introduced her to betting on the horses (there was a scene in the film at Ascot races), and she got quite involved in that and excited when her horses did well. To demonstrate how young I was at the time: during filming, she had her thirtieth birthday and the *Daily Mirror* did a big spread headed 'Sophia at 30'. I remember being amazed that she was so old! I think she looks wonderful in *Arabesque*. Donen and Christopher Challis, the cinematographer (who won a BAFTA for his work on *Arabesque*), photographed her perfectly. Her first entrance is simply stunning, helped by a lovely musical theme written by Henry Mancini and the Christian Dior outfit.

Gregory Peck was lovely. Kind. Generous. There was never a sense that he was a star and I was playing such a tiny role. And professional to the core. He never ever complained about have to reshoot again and again the 'falling into the water' sequence.

On a major film, everyone involved in the filming gets a call-sheet that explains the requirements for the following day. For instance, the prop-man sees what props will be needed, the caterers are warned how many will need to be fed and, of course, the taxi-drivers have to know who to pick up and from where. For three glorious days, at the top of the call-sheet, under the heading, ARTISTS REQUIRED, there were typed three names: GREGORY PECK, SOPHIA LOREN and GORDON GRIFFIN. Oh my!

I noticed that some of the crew, having read the call-sheet, just threw them aside so I went around collecting them. Well, I needed proof that this was all real and not just a dream. Above my desk, as I write this, is the call-sheet, framed. A reminded of those heady days.

For some reason, I didn't get a credit on the film. Neither did a number of actors who played small to medium roles. I'm not sure why. But many years later I was in Albacete in Spain (don't ask!) rummaging around in a record shop and I came across a vinyl LP of the music from the film. There was Gregory Peck and Sophia Loren on the front and on the back, a cast list where I got my credit. I bought the album, of course.

It's not one of Mancini's most famous scores but I think it's terrific. Not as commercial as his previous movie, *Charade,* but more sophisticated with a definite 'Arab' feel.

When I see the film now, I can barely recognise myself. I look so young. More like a schoolboy than a university student. I remember coming home from the final day's shooting (I had one more day on the film post-synchronising my dialogue) thinking how lucky I was. Fifteen months learning my craft at one of the best reps in the country and then appearing in a major movie even before I'd done a TV role. One of the extras who was also travelling on the train back to London came and sat opposite me.

"I hope you don't mind me saying this," she said, leaning forward conspiratorially, "But I am psychic. And I see a very successful career ahead for you."

I thanked her very much but took her prediction with a pinch of salt. I knew that I had a lot of hard work ahead of me. I had no idea where my career was going to take me. But I did recognise that I'd got off to a pretty good start.

Chapter 9

I had always been a fan of the actress Gwen Watford, so I was thrilled when I discovered that she was playing the lead in one of my first television plays. It was called *Take Care of Madam* and it was an episode in the *Blackmail* series. It was mostly set in a hairdresser's and I played Roger, a young hairdresser. It was a small part but at least I'd be working with the wonderful Miss Watford.

I arrived for the first rehearsal at a gymnasium in Lambs Conduit Street in Holborn. I tentatively put my head round the door. At the other end of the vast room some people were hovering around a tea urn. One of them looked towards the door and strode across the room towards me. It was Gwen Watford. She smiled and said, "We're just having a cup of tea. Come and join us." I knew she'd be lovely. And she was.

Suddenly, I was getting quite a lot of television roles. I played Robin, a young servant, in *The Canterbury Tales* (*The Miller's Tale*) for the BBC and a rather dramatic part in *Z Cars* playing a young bedridden guy who sees a murder from his bedroom window. It was a very good part and because the schedule was so tight, there wasn't a lot of time to learn the lines. Luckily, I played someone who was bedridden so I had no moves to learn. James Ellis was a regular in the series. He played PC Bert Lynch. In one scene he had to interview me in my bedroom. He had his script on the bed and when the camera was on me, he'd look at his next line and when the camera was on him again, he'd say it!

I was also fitting in stage work too. In Palmers Green in North London, a church hall had been converted into a theatre in the 1930s. It was called appropriately, The Intimate. Repertory seasons ran there from time to time. Sir John

Clements ran one such and among the actors who performed there over the years were David Bowie and Roger Moore.

In the 1960s, the writer and radio stalwart, Ernest Dudley, decided to take over The Intimate Theatre presenting classy productions with, where possible, big name performers. They even played Shakespeare. I didn't see it but Charlie Chester showed his Bottom there! I played Mr Elton in Jane Austen's *Emma* and then I played Tom Prior (a part made famous by Leslie Howard) in *Outward Bound*. The play tells of a group of people on a ship. What you don't know until well into the play is that they are all dead and they all have to go before The Examiner/Captain who will decide whether they go to heaven or hell. The Examiner in the Palmer's Green production was the film actor and television personality, Jimmy Hanley. He was a delight. In my final dramatic confrontation with him in the play, he had to show me a newspaper article. With a serious expression, he handed it to me. Every night when I opened it, there were pictures of naked women. I had to keep a straight face. He always had a twinkle in his eye. I liked him very much.

My first show at Palmer's Green was *Salad Days*, the charming and very English musical by Julian Slade and Dorothy Reynolds. I played PC Boot. It was my first professional musical but I had no solo singing to do. It was a very happy company, both onstage and off. There was a charming carpenter called Bob and during the *Look at Me I'm Dancing* number, the director wanted to fill the stage with as many people as possible, all dancing enthusiastically to the magic piano. The director wanted Bob to help out by coming onstage dressed as a bishop in gaiters etc., and join in the dancing. Bob was reluctant at first but he was such a good sport that he joined us onstage for the number, albeit a little self-consciously. He had a lovely gravelly London accent and when we went to the pub afterwards, he was the 'life and soul' with lots of lovely jokes and stories. One day, he told us that he'd like to be an actor. Don't forget this was the 1960s and someone with such a strong London accent was unlikely to make it very far. Well, only a few years later, he was playing the leading role in Brecht's *Man is Man* at the Royal Court. His name was Bob Hoskins.

Quite a few years later, I was cast in *Two Stars for Comfort*, by John Mortimer, adapted for radio for the BBC World Service. When the script arrived, I was delighted to see that Bob Hoskins was playing the main part. I had decided that, when there was a suitable break, I'd go up to him and remind him of our time together on *Salad Days*.

On the first day, we were due to read through the play before recording it. It was quite a big cast and we were seated in a circle waiting to start but Bob hadn't arrived. He was late and rushed in, eventually, full of apologies so I didn't get a chance to talk to him before the read-through. Halfway through the reading, we stopped for a coffee break and he came bounding over to me. "Hello, mate," he said giving me a hug. "How lovely to see you again."

Many years after that I was in the 'Acton Hilton' (that was the name we gave to the high-rise block that comprised floors of rehearsal rooms for BBC shows). Sit-coms and high drama were all rehearsed here. At the time I was rehearsing a children's book programme called *A Good Read* (not to be confused with the radio series of the same name). It was a fascinating programme to do for not only did I talk to camera and act in sketches but I got to interview children's writers, Jan Mark and Leon Garfield. A new departure for me.

On another floor at the same time, Anthony Hopkins was rehearsing *Othello* in BBC TV's ambitious Shakespeare series. Bob Hoskins was Iago. What an amazing career Bob had had and what a crowning achievement to play one of the great Shakespearean roles. I was telling the cast and crew of *A Good Read* about my experiences working with Bob.

One day, I was sitting with my cast and crew in the canteen and Bob walked in. Someone said rather disparagingly, I thought, *Oh, there's your friend, Bob Hoskins.* I just carried on with my meal. If I had passed his table on my out, I might have gone up and reminded him that years ago we had worked together. I noticed him choose his food and take his tray to his table at the other end of the room from where we were sitting. He had just put down his tray and was about to sit down when he looked around the room. He saw me, did a double take, and came bounding over.

"Gordon," he boomed. "What are you doing here?"

What an absolutely lovely man he was!

One final Palmer's Green anecdote. In *Salad Days* (or *Salad Daze* as I called it), there was a lovely guy in it called Roy. He was in his late 50s I'd guess and had had a very long career in rep. He was a very reliable actor with impeccable comedy timing. He was rather camp and a delightful company member. Everyone loved Roy. Some years later, I was heading toward my local underground station, and there he was! I rushed up to him and gave him a big hug.

"Roy. It's great to see you!"

Except it wasn't Roy! He looked so like him but as soon as he started to talk, I knew it wasn't him. I was so embarrassed.

"I'm so sorry," I blushed. "I thought you were someone else!"

He smiled a charming smile and said, "Don't apologise. I enjoyed it!"

After Palmer's Green, I went to do three plays at Westcliff Rep. I played Adhemar, the lover, in Sardou's *Let's Get a Divorce* and Will Roper in *A Man for All Season* opposite Jill Shilling as Margaret (coincidentally, Jill and I were to repeat our performances in an unconnected production on BBC radio). I also got to sing solo for the first time as Snodgrass, one of the Pickwickians, in the musical, *Pickwick*, which somehow, we managed to get on with only a week's rehearsal.

Someone, who saw a rather shambolic rehearsal of the dance numbers, said that it looked more like a musical version of *The Miracle Worker!*

Working as assistant stage manager was a very keen local girl called Rita Craven. She worked hard backstage but relished getting onstage in walk-on roles. I remember her as a very funny policeman (with moustache) in *Let's Get a Divorce.* A few years later, she had changed her first name to Gemma. When I saw her playing opposite Bob Hoskins in the

BBC's hugely successful series, *Pennies from Heaven*, it struck me that from backstage to stardom for some wasn't so big a leap!

I carried on doing TV roles. I look at the list, the ones I can remember, and because we didn't then have recording devices, I have no idea what I did in them. I see a character's name and a play's title, and it means nothing. Of course, some series were recorded and eventually came out many years later. One such was *A Family at War*. I played Doug, a young rear-gunner who was a nice guy who (like so many) comes to a sticky end. We filmed in a real Lancaster bomber. It was supposed to be airborne but Tim Jones, the director, worked out a way of filming that made it look as though we were flying. The DVD of *A Family at War* came out exactly thirty years after I had played the part. It was so weird watching (possibly for the first time) that young actor who was me. It was strange because I could look at him as though he was another actor.

As I watched, a lot of the experience of the filming came back to me. I remember I had to learn a song I'd not heard of at that point called *She Wore a Little Jacket of Blue*. Doug had to sing it on the flight over Germany. It's the last you heard or saw of the poor lad. I'd never ever heard that song before, until years later, I did the narration for a DVD on the life of Alma Cogan and, during the documentary, there was Alma singing it.

I remember for different reasons my time on a now-forgotten soap called *The Newcomers*. It was a twice-weekly saga about a London family that relocates to East Anglia. It starred a very warm, friendly Australian singer/actress, Maggie Fitzgibbon as the mum and fellow-Geordie, Alan Browning, as her husband. Judy Geeson played their daughter and Jeremy Bullock their son. In my storyline, I am involved in a wages-snatch and because I looked a bit like Jeremy, at an identity-parade, he is mistaken for the culprit. The schedule was so tight that, although the Tuesday episode was recorded, the Friday episode was live. Is there anything scarier than that?

On the live Friday episode that I was involved in, the programme started. My character is by now on the run after the robbery with my colleague and co-robber. The scene is in a coffee bar. My character is nervous and is being told to calm down by his fellow villain who was played by Jonathan Dennis. The first scene of the episode was in the local pub. Across the studio floor, I could see the scene happening live! I was supposed to face forward towards the camera with Jonathan leaning over me. Our scene was the third of the episode and we were in our places. After the pub scene, there was a short bit of tele-cine of the actually wages-snatch and of me driving the get-away car. Then comes the café scene that we were waiting for. For some reason, the film didn't come on. For seconds, there was a blank screen and then I was given a frantic cue to start our scene. Luckily, we were in place and ready but I was so thrown by the lack of film. I kept thinking, *This doesn't make sense.* What I should have been thinking was, *What do I say first?* I also saw to the right of the camera, a monitor on which my face was looking worried. I was in character, of course, but I remember thinking that everyone at home will be watching that picture. Well, I was so thrown by all this, I forgot my words. My mind went blank. Because I was playing a nervous guy, I was able to bluster and stutter. Jonathan was brilliant and calmly got us back on script but I have never been more terrified as an actor.

But my career was jogging along quite nicely. I wasn't setting the world on fire but I was being kept busy, improving my skills and making new friends. Then, in 1968, I took what was to be the first stepping-stone that would, eventually, lead me to recording audiobooks. I was offered my first radio part. I was to play 16-year-old Billy, Mrs Dales' grandson, in the iconic radio series *The Dales* (formerly *Mrs Dales' Diary*). Mrs Dale was played by the great Jessie Matthews so that meant my grandmother was to be Jessie Matthews! But, more importantly, it was to open the door for me to a world where the 'voice' was one's most important attribute. I didn't know it then but this was not only the beginning of my radio career but also the beginning of a whole new world for me.

Chapter 10

Radio. A great medium for an actor. It doesn't matter what you look like. You can play any part and as long as the listener believes it, then it works. Anyone can play anything. Here was I, an actor in my early 20s, playing a 16-year-old. Even though I looked young for my age, there is no way that I could have played Billy onstage but I had a young-sounding voice and by very slightly lightening it, I could convincingly sound like a 16-year-old.

Interestingly, there was, at that time, a successful television series starring Wendy Craig. One of the many, it seemed, where she was bringing up her family. In one of these series, her youngest son was fifteen. So successful was the series that the BBC decided to do it on radio. The same actors were assembled for the broadcasts. The fifteen-year-old actor was totally convincing on television as you could see that he was fifteen. However, on the radio, where you only had his voice, he sounded so much older. He had a deep gravelly voice that didn't convey a schoolboy at all. So here you had a situation where a real fifteen-year-old sounded unconvincing and I, someone in his twenties, sounded completely authentic.

I don't remember ever having had an audition for *The Dales* or even meeting anyone regarding the part of Billy. A friend, actor Stanley Bates, had suggested me to the producers and one day I got a call from one of them. She explained that Stanley had suggested me and then continued to explain the character and schedule. She asked me what I had been doing and I remember trying to sound young without changing my voice too much. It must have worked because the contract appeared in the post a few days later.

That same producer, who had interviewed me over the telephone, welcomed me on my first day. She surprisingly warned me against getting too involved with Jessie Matthews as she'll 'talk you to death'. I thought that was a strange thing to say. I was, in fact, looking forward to meeting Jessie and if she talked nonstop, I'd be only too happy to listen. And so it proved. I liked her very much. She had her demons, was a little eccentric and odd at times. But she was a great big star, one of the greatest we have even produced. When she played on Broadway, she stopped the traffic. Fred Astaire pleaded with her to do a film with him, her films were huge hits. She was now in her 60s, matronly, not at all the gamine dancer of her youth but I loved to sit beside her and get her talking about her life.

At this time, she'd been asked to write an autobiography. She wasn't too keen and because she couldn't get around to actually writing pages of notes, her publishers gave her a tape-recorder which she was able to turn on and talk into. The publishers thought this would be one way of getting down her life story. As she remembered each incident or anecdote, the idea was that she would be able to switch on the tape and talk into the machine.

I thought that this was a good idea, but she told me that she found it trying.

"Trying?" I remember asking her. "Isn't it interesting to recall those exciting days?"

"Oh no," she shuddered. "No. I don't want to remember. There are too many painful memories."

How sad that this great star couldn't even look back on her huge career and recall the good times she had had.

The cast of *The Dales* was friendly. I bonded particularly with Aline Waites who played my mother, Gwen, and with Judy Bennett, who played my little brother, Phil. In those days, small boys were often played by actresses who specialised in doing their voices. There were a small number who played most of the little boy's roles and Judy was one. She enjoyed the work but longed to play an adult. Later, she auditioned for and got the part of a little girl (at least, it wasn't a boy) in the rival radio soap, *The Archers*. The part was Shula and Judy grew up with the part. So she got her wish. As I write this, she's still in *The Archers*, playing an adult! Incidentally, Billy's first girlfriend in *The Dales*, Cherry, was played by Pat Gallimore. She also defected to the competition and has for a long time now been Pat Archer.

My first scene as Billy was with the actor Bill Treacher, who I think played a garage mechanic. Although I'd done radio training at drama school, this was the real thing and I mentioned quietly to Bill that this was my debut as a radio actor. Without making a fuss, he told me the best place to stand and gave me a few tips about how best to hold the script and turn over pages without making a noise. It all went swimmingly. I'd done it. I was away and confident. Bill Treacher went into *EastEnders*, where he was the first actor to be cast and was with the series for eleven years. Nice man.

Billy was a typical middle-class sixteen-year-old. This was the late 1960s but this was very much family listening. There was no way that young Billy was going to get up to no good. No drugs, no sex, no controversy. But I was having a lovely time doing *The Dales* until it was announced that the series was going to end. It had started as *Mrs Dales' Diary* in 1948 with Ellis Powell as Mary Dale and that wonderful Shakespearean actor James Dales as… er… James Dale. In 1963, it re-emerged as *The Dales,* with Jessie as Mary and Charles Simon as Dr James Dale. I think the idea was to make it buzzier and more up-to-date but it was always rather cosy and I think that's why people liked it. When I was a youngster, I remember rushing home from school to hear it. For me, growing up in the northeast, it was exciting. Parkwood Hill was a suburb of London, one of Mrs Dales' daughters was an actress. It was a world that was so different from my own. It was a slightly surreal experience when I walked into the studio on that first day, except, of course, I used to listen to *Mrs Dales' Diary*, not *The Dales*.

It was sad that after all those years, it was finally going to end. But on April 25th, 1969, the curtain came down on this iconic series. I was in the very last episode. Because it was the end of the series, there was a lot of publicity and the story even made news bulletins and photographs of the cast were on the front pages of most of the newspapers the following day.

In those days, it wasn't easy to record programmes from the radio, so if I didn't catch an episode, then I missed hearing it! But I wanted very much to hear the final programme. I was at the time filming in Brighton on a movie called *All the Right Noises*. The stars were Olivia Hussey, Tom Bell and Judy Carne. I'd just filmed one of my scenes in a café off the promenade in Brighton and I had a little time before I was next needed. I found a bench near the café but out of earshot and turned on my little transistor radio. Good timing. I should be able to hear the whole episode. I was just about to start to listen when Tom Bell came over and sat down beside me to have a cigarette.

"What are you listening to?" Tom asked me.

Rather self-consciously I muttered that it was the last episode of *The Dales* and that I was in it.

Amazingly, he said, "Oh, turn it up then. I love *The Dales*."

If you remember Tom Bell (fine actor), the rather tough image he projected didn't quite fit with someone who wanted to hear about the goings on in the Dales' family!

My particular friend on *The Dales* was Aline Waites who, as I mentioned before, played my mum. Because I was nearly ten years older than the part I was playing, Aline could never in real-life have been my mother although even to this day we call each other 'mum' and 'son'.

Aline, at the time, was running an Old Tyme Music Hall above a pub in Hampstead and she suggested I come and do a number. As I have said before, I love singing, but only for myself. My voice sounded great in the shower. I play the piano and the way I relaxed (and still do) was to sit at my piano and sing away to myself: show songs, Gershwin, the Beatles. But actually getting up in front of an audience? Er, no thanks.

Aline was nothing if not persistent. My brother, meanwhile, had told me of a shop in North Shields that was closing down. Amazingly, this shop just sold sheet music and he thought there might be some interesting stuff there. The next time I was in the northeast, I popped into the shop. It was dusty and dark, and there were indeed piles and piles of old sheet music. I searched through them and came away with a pile of musical scores and songs.

When I got home, I worked my way through them. It was in a very old music hall book that was yellow with age and falling to pieces, that I came across a saucy number called *Oh, Amelia!* about a young sailor who goes off on his honeymoon and comes back looking 'like the ruins of Pompeii'. It was very funny and slightly risqué but it was an authentic music hall song, and, even better, no one seemed to know it.

Eventually, I said to Aline, "Look, I have found this number. I will come to rehearsals and sing it for you. If you think I am not up to scratch then you must tell me. I won't be offended at all. I'd prefer not to make a fool of myself."

I went to the rehearsal and the song went better than I could have expected. Everyone found it hilariously funny. So I was to perform it on a bill in Hampstead.

I loved *Oh, Amelia!* It became my sort of signature song and I performed it everywhere. I sang it dressed as a sailor and even added a few dance steps. This was just for fun, of course. I was (I kept reminding myself) an actor not a musicals man. Nevertheless, on the second night, there was a knock on my dressing room door. Who am I kidding? There was a knock on 'the' dressing room door! We all shared one. A small, birdlike lady asked if she could have a word. She told me how much she'd enjoyed my song and went on: "I have written a musical and I'd like you to be in it!"

The lady was Betty Lawrence, musical director of the famous Players Theatre and the musical was based on the Crummles' chapters of *Nicholas Nickleby*. The great James Hayter (born to play Dickens with that fruity 'exceedingly good cakes' voice) was to play Crummles. "Would you like to play Smike?"

Goodness, what was this? Me, being offered a part in a musical? How did that happen? It took me about two minutes to say yes. The show was called *Step into the Limelight* and it was to open at the Palace Theatre in Manchester. It was all slightly unreal. I was happy that Aline's confidence in me was justified. And, of course, I had a very soft spot from then on for *Oh, Amelia!*

Chapter 11

Step into the Limelight was not a success. The performances were fine and the music had a lot of charm but it just didn't hang together. The show was essentially small scale and would have suited smaller, more intimate theatres than the vast Palace Theatre in Manchester and the Hippodrome in Bristol. But it was a positive experience and I made friends, and I was now confident in auditioning for musicals. I had auditioned for musicals before, of course, but I had never expected to get them. In those days, I auditioned for everything, went for every interview. For example, I did countless auditions and recalls for *Hair* and I auditioned for the original London cast of the Bock and Harnick musical, *She Loves Me*. I went along to the theatre and sang my audition song (*Don't Marry Me* from Rodgers' and Hammerstein's *Flower Drum Song*) and was amazed when I got a recall.

A week or so later, I sang my song again. A very nice American walked through the auditorium to the stage. I leaned forward to hear him say how much he'd enjoyed my audition. I was amazed and thrilled. He then introduced me to the choreographer. Well, I am skilled at a few things, but dancing, sadly, is not one of my strong points. At least, I can dance but I can't do the instant choreography expected at an audition.

I obviously looked alarmed and this nice guy said, "Don't worry, it's really not difficult."

The choreographer did a sort of spin and a couple of simple steps and my mind went blank. I tried but couldn't reproduce what she had just done. The friendly man thanked me courteously and I fled knowing I'd blown it. The nice, encouraging man, I learned afterwards, was the great Hal

Prince! Hal Prince, the great Broadway producer, who has over twenty Tony awards!

I went to see the show and Gregory Phillips who played 'my' part was very good but all the time I watched him, I thought, *I could do that.* The dancing was minimal.

I was auditioning for a Palladium pantomime and handed over my music to the pianist. I was going to sing *If I Ever Fall in Love Again* from *The Crooked Mile* but the pianist took one look at the music and said in a shocked voice, "I can't play this!" as though I was trying to trick him. It's not that easy to play I know. But, hell, he was being paid to play for the auditions. I sang a different song instead (*Opposites* from Lionel Bart's *Blitz*). I had an eclectic repertoire.

But now that I'd been in a big musical, albeit one in which I did only a little singing, perhaps I was ready to perform in a big show.

In the meantime, I did more television series, more repertory and (happily) more music hall.

Aline had set up shop in Mother Red Cap (and later, The Pindar of Wakefield) in Camden Town and she lured some very big names to perform for her. One of the funniest was Lynda Marshal. We all enjoyed being on a 'bill' with her. She kept us in stitches and the audiences loved her. So it was rather surprising that she became famous, after she had changed her name to Lynda La Plante, for serious drama. A bestselling novelist, she created *Prime Suspect,* a hugely successful, ground-breaking television series that starred Helen Mirren as DCI Jane Tennison.

For Aline, I trotted out my trusted *Oh Amelia!* And had fun searching out other suitable songs for the shy, put upon character I'd created for the shows. Songs like *She Pushed Me into the Parlour* and *Put me amongst the Girls*, often duetting with the wonderful Jacqueline Clarke. The audiences entered into the spirit and we all had a good time.

Of course, the Players Theatre was the music hall mecca and I got a call to go and audition for them. Betty Lawrence, who had written the music for *Step into the Limelight*, had put in a good word. I'd been to the Players as a member of the audience many times. It was always such a fun night out and I was in awe of the talent onstage. Well, *Oh Amelia!* was trotted out yet again! And lo and behold, I was offered my first 'bill' there.

The Players had a huge archive of music hall songs and certain performers there had exclusive rights to performing their own particular numbers. Woe betide anyone who even considered singing a song that 'belonged' to one of the Players' regulars. No one had ever heard of *Oh Amelia!* They didn't have a copy of it in their extensive library so I was to introduce Amelia and my 'sailor boy' to the Players.

At the end of each show after the individual acts, there was a scena: songs with a particular theme or by the same composer. My first scena was a Gilbert and Sullivan medley which was heavenly although the formidable choreographer, Doreen Hermitage, had a few 'eyes to heaven' moments trying to teach me the steps. Bless her though, over the months, she recognised that I would be fine. I just needed to go home and practise. I'd get there in the end but I just couldn't do 'instant' chorography.

Being a member of the Players company meant that some of us regulars got slots on the hugely popular BBC television show *The Good Old Days* which was recorded on Sundays at the City Varieties in Leeds. I was lucky enough to do two shows there with Leonard Sachs as the loquacious chairman. I backed the great music hall legend Tessie O'Shea, and also Sandie Shaw who sang a Marie Lloyd medley.

I sometimes felt a bit of a fraud being in such exalted company but they were very kind to me and I performed at the Players on and off for two years. I even did one of their famous traditional pantomimes which were charming Victorian affairs beautifully designed by Reggie Woolley. Reggie was able to transform the tiny stage (the backstage area was virtually non-existent) into a magical place with beautiful painting and clever lighting.

Reggie was a stalwart of the Players and one of his many claims to fame was that he commissioned Sandy Wilson to write a little show for his Players Theatre Company. It was called *The Boy Friend* and when it transferred from the Players to the West End, it ran for over 2,000 performances, making it one of the longest running shows in the West End at that time. It starred Anne Rogers and when a Broadway production was planned, it was expected that Anne would head the cast there. But Vida Hope the director wanted Anne to stay with the show in London. Someone else would have to play her part in New York. Hattie Jacques, a Players stalwart, suggested a young singer who, although she'd appeared in variety and in pantomime, had never done a musical. The Broadway producers took Hattie's advice. The singer she recommended was Julie Andrews!

My time performing solo numbers at the Players was well spent; I gained huge confidence in 'playing' to an audience. I learned about timing from the wonderful chairmen/masters of ceremonies there and I enjoyed the camaraderie of the company and the après-show drinks in the bar at the back of the auditorium. The Players was also a great place to meet friends.

I was very fond of musical theatre. I still am. I went to see everything I could. I remember being bowled over by *Godspell* at the Wyndham's Theatre. Funny, irreverent and in the end, very moving. Everyone I knew wanted to be in the tour. This would be the very first tour ever of the show. It hadn't been playing in London very long (starring David Essex and Jeremy Irons) and the idea of performing this vibrant show on its first outing around the UK was something that a lot of us wanted to do.

As always, I went enthusiastically to the first audition and it seemed to me that a music hall style song would suit the show so what should I sing for the audition? Enter yet again, *Oh Amelia!* The American production team loved it. I got a recall. And then another. At one, the third I think, I had to present a parable in any way I chose. I did *The Good Samaritan* as a stand-up comedian. Lots of puns which was up my street. It didn't take me long to write but I wondered whether my jokes might be a bit too English. Apparently not. They laughed a lot.

The final audition was a tough one. There are ten people in *Godspell*, five female and five male (including the Jesus and Judas characters) and at that final audition there were twenty of us. When we arrived, we were told who we were paired with, which meant that I met the person who was up for the same part as I was. It was a shocking moment. He was one of the most successful young West End performers. Unlike me, he'd played leads in a number of West End musicals. He was charming and had a lovely voice.

This long audition consisted of us playing 'get to know you' games and then someone from the stalls would say, pointing to say one of the girls, "You. Sing something." Or to one of the guys, "You. Tell us a joke. Make us laugh." It was all getting a bit frustrating. How long were we going to be there? We did as we were told. We all wanted this job. One of the guys who was auditioning said that he had to go as he had to get to York where he was currently performing and he had a show that evening. The producers weren't very sympathetic. But they had no choice but to release him.

We poured out of the theatre and some of us went for a coffee near the theatre. I think we were deflated. I wasn't feeling confident. I didn't think that I had had a chance to show what I could do. My only hope was that they would consider all my auditions and not just this last one.

I knew the company-manager of the current West End production of *Godspell* and he asked where I'd be later in the day in case there was any news. I gave him the name and number of a friend I was going to see. I needed a drink.

I'd not been at my friend's flat for long when Tony, the company-manager, phoned. "It's yours," was all he said.

"What?" I yelled back at him.

"You got the part."

I thought I would faint with joy. I wanted the job so much. A year's work. A great though controversial show.

I phoned my mother who was delighted but distracted. She had just heard at that moment that my brother and his wife had had a baby boy. She was a grandmother for the second time. Later, she phoned me back. When could she see the show?

"Hang on, I haven't started rehearsing it yet."

But this was to be an amazing tour. In those days it was unusual for a show to play more than a couple of weeks in one place but *Godspell* was going to play ten weeks in Glasgow, twelve in Edinburgh, five weeks in Bristol etc. But how exciting was this? The very first date was to be at the Theatre Royal in Newcastle. My hometown. My home theatre. I knew my friends and family would give the show a great send off. This was the most exciting moment of my career so far.

Godspell opens with the cast as philosophers declaiming. I was Socrates. I was the first person to sing. One by one the philosophers belt out their theories, eventually they are all singing one on top of the other. Chaos. There is noise. And from the back of the auditorium appears John the Baptist singing, *Prepare Ye the way of the Lord.* We disappear during the noise and emerge from the 'babble' bouncing onstage in our clown costumes singing *When wilt thou save the people?*

So there I was, on the first night of the first tour standing in the centre of the stage at the beautiful Theatre Royal Newcastle, singing the first lines of the show (as Socrates): *Wherefore, O men of Athens, I say to you...* What a moment. My family and friends were in the auditorium I knew. This was it. This is what I'd worked for. It wasn't the West End but it was the most important theatre in my life. I was particularly pleased that my dad was in the audience to see what I'd achieved. He never understood why I wanted to be an actor. I don't think he ever really believed I'd make a go of it. He wanted either my brother Andrew or me to take over the family business. But, to be fair to him, he never ever argued about it. He recognised that I had to give it a go. When eventually my dad gave up his Byker fish shop, my parents bought a newsagent's shop in Monkseaton, Whitley Bay and my mum used to tell me that my dad would say to the customers, rather proudly, "Did you see Gordon on television last night?"

The production of *Godspell* was overseen by the writer, John-Michael Tebelak but the director was one of the original cast members who didn't understand our British sense of humour. The show consists of a series of parables and the actors have to interpret them in whatever way they choose that is entertaining and fun. He didn't understand much of my punning, my verbal humour. He much preferred my fellow-actor, Jack's, more physical comedy. When he started to give Jack a couple of bits of business that should have been mine, I made a fuss and even considered leaving the cast.

But on the first night at Newcastle with a packed audience, I got my laughs. My taking a stance had been justified. After the huge ovation at the end of the show, the director did admit that he was wrong. He was still mystified as to what the audience found funny in my performance. For the Newcastle show, I even slotted in a punch line to a particular sketch in a broad Geordie accent. It brought the house down. And did every night of the run. I had to change that line depending where we were playing.

Godspell ran for a year. The cast included a couple of young performers fresh from drama school who went on to become television and theatre 'names': Lesley Joseph and Susie Blake.

Forty years after *Godspell*, Susie and I were reunited in a recording of the musical, *Something's Afoot*. At the first rehearsal for the recording we fell into each other arms and just carried on from where we'd left off!

Because *Godspell* was controversial and had a religious theme, we got a lot of publicity. We did a number of radio and television interviews, and forums with church groups. We were entertained by bishops and other religious leaders who, in the main, thought *Godspell* was a good thing. But not everyone did. During a performance at Bournemouth, a man walked very slowly down to the front of the stage and then (again slowly) walked up the steps leading onto the stage. We were all in the middle of a lively number at the time. This man lifted his programme into the air, and very slowly, tore it up and let the pieces fall onto the floor of the stage. Wonderful Susie danced down towards him, still in character and, putting her arm through his, danced him offstage.

Whilst in Bournemouth we had two contrasting invitations. The first was to spend Sunday afternoon with Lord Montagu of Beaulieu. He'd invited the whole cast and crew but Jess Conrad, the handsome ex-pop star who was playing Jesus, had another engagement which seemed to disappoint his lordship.

Nevertheless, we sat by his pool and later had a personal tour of the house by Lord Montagu himself followed by a nursery tea in his private apartments.

By complete contrast, on another Sunday, we were invited to do the show at the Albany Prison on the Isle of Wight. We had been told that this was a modern prison and that it held some notorious prisoners.

Sunday afternoon, when we were to perform the show, was the prisoner's recreational period, when they could go outside and play football and get some exercise. We'd been warned that if it was a sunny day, we might not have a full house.

I was a glorious summer day!

After lunch with the Governor and staff, we were shown the large gym where we were to perform. We had to go through many locked doors and gates and instead of using keys, the warders opened them with plastic cards. Now it's the usual way to get into hotel rooms but at the time, I'd not seen this impressive operation.

We were shown into the locker rooms where we were to change. Suddenly, I felt claustrophobic. There were no doors on the loos. No privacy. I could understand the reasoning for the lack of doors but it was a rather chilling sight.

Any doubts that we might have had about there being only a small audience were quickly dispelled. The gym was packed. We had a 'captive' audience and it seemed that they were buzzing with excitement and anticipation.

The only thing that was cut from the show for this performance was the opening of Act Two where Lesley would normally go through the audience singing her 'vamp' number *Turn Back O Man*. During this number, she'd sometimes ruffle a man's hair or sit on his knee. For this performance she sang it as seductively as usual, but from the stage.

The audience was amazing. They cheered, they laughed. They roared at any references to 'sinners ending up in jail'. But we reckoned that at the end, which should be very moving, they would find that funny too. But they didn't. They were so quiet and the silence was so powerful.

When we came leaping onto the stage for the curtain call, they went crazy. Yelling and shouting and cheering. We were all moved.

When we were 'released' after the show, we were all silent and thoughtful. We all took deep breaths to inhale fresh air hoping to get rid of that distinctive 'prison' smell that was in our nostrils.

On the boat going back to the mainland we were a silent and reflective bunch. I have never forgotten that show and I am sure that the others haven't either.

Godspell generated a lot of 'groupies', fans who often followed the show from place to place. They must have paid a fortune on train fares alone. We all had our particular fans and signing autographs after the show was a long process, but of course, we did it willingly and happily.

There was often not much time between a matinee and an evening show. In Bristol, I think it was, they were calling the 'half' for the evening show (that's thirty-five minutes before curtain up) as we were coming offstage. From the matinee! But at Newcastle, we had a bit longer, and I'd volunteered to go across the road to get sandwiches and coffee for the others. As I was the only one of the cast who came out, I was bombarded. It was quite alarming. I was surrounded by a gang of over-excited girls, some of whom wanted me to sign varies body parts. At one point, I extracted myself and made a dash for the café. They chased after me. Eventually, I had to plead with them to calm down. I promised I'd sign all their programmes but I needed to get coffees for the cast first. And that's what happened. A bit scary though.

The tour of *Godspell*, though not the West End production, was presented by H M Tennents, a company famous for lavish productions with star names and for years Hugh 'Binkie' Beaumont was in charge. He had a fearsome reputation and ruled the West End for years. He fell out with his two closest collaborators, John Gielgud and Noel Coward, and altogether, he seemed to me a rather scary man. I'd not met him, of course, but while we were playing at the Birmingham Hippodrome, he came to see the show and rather surprisingly loved it (maybe because it was making Tennents a lot of money).

Afterwards, he had arranged for us all to have dinner at a smart restaurant and I was horrified when I saw that I was to sit next to him. What would I say to him? Would I be in awe and tongue-tied and make a fool of myself? In the event, he was delightful company. He had genuinely loved the show and talked enthusiastically about it. He had wonderful stories and seemed to me to be self-effacing and rather sweet.

I didn't know that he was ill and was shocked when, only a few weeks later, I read that he had died. I was particularly shocked that this rather charming old man (as he had appeared to me) was only sixty-four at his death.

Godspell, like *Hair,* was very much of its time. I have not seen a modern production of it that worked. The music is still great (Stephen Schwartz), but somehow, the innocence and naivety these days seems to be 'stuck on' and 'sent up'. In productions of *Hair*, the cast seem to 'act' at being hippies. We didn't need to act it, we 'were'.

I wasn't particular religious then (I am not at all now) but I always found 'the Last Supper' sequence very moving, where (at the end) we take the body of 'Jesus' through the audience singing *Prepare ye the way of the Lord.* When this song segues into *Long Live God*, it always got to us. And to the audience too, I think. When we finally ended our year's run, at the Royal Court Theatre in Liverpool, knowing we were breaking up our 'family', hardly any of us could sing. Even writing this now, I can recall very clearly, that the tears were rolling down our cheeks. When we came onstage for our calls, I have never heard such cheering. It went on and on and on. A lot of the shows' 'followers' were there to see us off. It was an incredibly draining experience. I remember us all sitting in the dressing room afterwards – just sitting there staring into the mirror, not wanting to take off the makeup. That would mean it really was the end.

Actually, it wasn't quite the end for me. The cast that was taking over from us was due to open at the Kings Theatre in Southsea and I joined them for that one date (three weeks I think) because one of their cast wasn't yet free.

Surprisingly, I wasn't playing my part, but I could have played any role. I knew every song and everyone's lines.

Before I'd gone off on tour with *Godspell*, I had been approached by *Play School*, the iconic BBC television programme for young children, asking me to consider being a regular presenter. My policy was usually to say 'Yes'. A presenter of *Play School* was something I thought I could do!

I presented five programmes with my co-host, Chloe Ashcroft who was a regular and was very helpful and kind to me and showed me the ropes. It was tight schedule. We'd record programme one on Monday morning, programme two on Monday afternoon, programme three on Tuesday morning etc. There was no autocue so before we started on the Monday, we had to know all the scripts: the songs, the stories and the presentation. I had some lines that could easily be 'double entendres' but the crew was very professional. Chloe, at one point, was making something with some twigs, then they cut to me, and I sang a song and then after the song, I had to look at the camera and say, "Shall we see what Chloe is doing with those twigs?" Not a particular funny line now, but at the time, I thought it was hilarious. But everyone kept a straight face. Consummate professionals. All of them.

Many years later, I was at the launch of the two-volume history of *Play School* by Paul R Jackson and I met Michael Bond, the creator of *Paddington Bear*. I wondered what he was doing there until he explained that he had been a cameraman on *Play School* and *Blue Peter* before *Paddington* took off. Not long ago, I recorded one of the books in his delightful *Pamplemousse* series which he wrote when he was well into his 80s. The writing is full of vitality – just like he was.

After my week of *Play School*, I was half-expecting to hear from the company with either a letter of rejection or more bookings. But I heard nothing. When *Godspell* came up, of course, I jumped at the chance.

Quite a few months into the run, I got a message from *Play School* with some dates for more programmes for me to record. I explained that as I'd not heard anything from them, I'd assumed that they didn't want me. I certainly couldn't wait around twiddling my thumbs for months. I was committed to a year's tour with *Godspell* so, regretfully, I had to turn the BBC down.

The producer wasn't pleased. But I had no contract. There were no guarantees in place. I wasn't too disappointed as I was having such a lovely time on tour but I was a bit miffed by their attitude.

When Paul Jackson was researching his *Play School* books, he contacted me and asked him to tell him about my experience. I emailed him about what had happened. I was surprised that my email appeared in the book exactly as I'd written it to him! He'd, in any case, seen correspondence of the incident and knew the story!

Incidentally, when I was getting to the end of my tour, I contacted the *Play School* producer saying I'd be back in London soon and wondering whether she'd still consider me as a presenter. I added that I'd be very happy to do more programmes. I got a curt reply. No.

The nearest we came to London with *Godspell* were the weeks we played over Christmas at the lovely Theatre Royal Brighton. Every night, it seemed some starry person was watching. Jess Conrad was playing Jesus and he knew everyone. And through Jess, I met Diana Dors and Dora Bryan. And, of course, my own friends jetted in from London to see the show too. One friend, Hugh, a northeast pal, came to see a Friday evening show. I'd organised a table for us afterwards at an Italian restaurant near the theatre. After the show, the two of us walked into the restaurant and (this has never happened before or since) the diners started to applaud. It was only then that I noticed that they had *Godspell* programmes on the tables beside them. I thanked the diners graciously and we were shown to our seats.

I said to Hugh as we sat down, "That's never happened to me before."

"What hasn't?"

I was still thrilled by what had happened. "That. People applauding as I came into the restaurant. It's like Sardi's. In New York!"

Hugh didn't know what I was talking about. Ah, well. There was no way I was going to get big-headed. Not with friends like Hugh around!

Chapter 12

After *Godspell* I went back into radio for a while. If I'd thought that they'd let me grow up, now that I was in my early thirties, I was wrong. I was still being cast as angst-ridden teenagers. But that played to my advantage when the BBC decided to do a four-part version of the whole of *Romeo and Juliet*. The older parts were played by stalwarts of the BBC Drama Repertory Company but the producer wanted Romeo and Juliet to be the ages they are in the play – Juliet is fifteen and Romeo sixteen. So, here was an angst-ridden teenager I was very happy to play.

This production was recorded onto cassette (ah! Cassettes – they play a big part in my story) and I was listening to it the other day. I do indeed sound very young. Young, confused and passionate.

I was a regular 'reader' for Radio 4's arts programme, *Kaleidoscope*. If a book were being discussed or reviewed, I'd be sent to the studio where the producer would describe briefly the plot of the book (if it were a novel) and I'd record extracts. It was incredibly good training for what was to come later.

I was, in fact, doing quite a lot of storytelling. As well as presenting the children's book programme on BBC Schools television, I had been guest storyteller on *Rainbow* and, of course, told stories on *Play School*. A lot of my radio work involved telling tales. And not just for the BBC.

In the early days of LBC, inexplicably, the powers-that-be decided to have a daily serial of fifteen minutes each weekday during Brian Hayes' popular phone-in programme. For those who don't remember him, Hayes was a wonderfully grumpy presenter who was often rude to his callers. It seemed eccentric even then to interrupt his show for a serialisation of a classic novel. I recorded two for this slot. Thomas Hardy's *The Trumpet Major* and Joseph Conrad's *The Planter of Malata*. I didn't realise it at the time but this was all leading me to the world of audiobooks, although they weren't called that then. They were usually referred to as 'talking books'.

Meanwhile, I had been cast as The Owl in David Wood's children's musical, *The Owl and the Pussycat Went to See...* I played it each Christmas season in and around London. We performed at the now demolished Westminster Theatre and also on a tour that saw me, once again, treading the hallowed boards on the Theatre Royal in Newcastle. Kids loved this show and when the Owl and Pussycat get married, the volume of noise from them was deafening.

For one of the productions of it, we had a new young producer. On the first night at Guildford (not strictly speaking 'night' as we played in the afternoons), I found a sweet note and a bottle of good champagne for me from that producer. That was a lovely surprise. It was an unexpected gesture and much appreciated. The producer was called Cameron Mackintosh. I wonder what became of him!

I wasn't one for having ambitions although I had always wanted work at the Festival Theatre at Chichester. I auditioned three years in a row in an attempt to do a season there. On the third occasion, I duly arrived at the West End theatre where the auditions were to be held and was introduced to the director of that season, Keith Michell. My audition pieces were the opening of *Little Malcolm and his Struggle against the Eunuchs* by David Halliwell and a piece of Fenton from Shakespeare's *The Merry Wives of Windsor*.

I know some people claim that, to succeed in the theatre one needs luck. I know some very lucky actors who have done well by being in the right place at the right time, but sometimes, it's just about auditioning and auditioning until you get the part. I was determined to get to Chichester, and if I had had to audition every year, I would have done. So, it wasn't luck that got me there. Keith liked my audition. I was in.

I was to play Metellus Cimber, the youngest of the conspirators in *Julius Caesar* directed by Peter Dews. Dews had directed *The Age of Kings* (his adaptation of the Shakespeare history plays) as well as the Roman plays (*The Spread of the Eagle*) for BBC Television. He was a brilliant man and one of the great authorities on Shakespeare.

Caesar was to be the third play in the season and I was joining the company for it. I arrived at the theatre for the first rehearsal and bumped into Terry Wale who was also joining for *Caesar*. We were informed at the stage door that the rehearsal was not at the theatre. It was at a rehearsal room quite a walk away. We'd not been told this so we dashed the half-mile or so to the rehearsal venue just as everyone was sitting in a large semi-circle getting ready to read the play.

I'd not met Dews at this point. There he stood like a benign though strict schoolmaster. I wish I could remember what his opening speech was like. I am sure it was witty and wise. I learned later that he had a wicked sense of humour and was, like me, a lover of puns.

There were a lot of us. It was a huge cast and, as I said, only Terry and I had not been in the first two productions, although Terry had worked with Peter a couple of times, not least on *The Age of Kings*.

Peter's party piece, I discovered, was being able to remember everyone's name, however large the company. So, he began to introduce his company. He indicated the actor or stage management or crew member and then named them. It was very impressive. He started on his right and worked left. I was about three-quarters of the way along the row. He indicated me with his hands and looked blank. Everyone waited. Silence.

"Er…"

He was struggling. At last he said, "No. Sorry. You'll have to tell me!"

Not a great start to my Chichester sojourn!

For Peter Dews' production of *Julius Caesar* we wore Puritan costumes. For the actual murder of Caesar we conspirators wore white floor length gowns. I was the

97

youngest of them so Peter had the others 'blood' me, so that at the end of the murder sequence my white gown was covered in gore. Messy. The very nice Nigel Stock was Caesar. And also in the cast was Vernon Dobtcheff.

Vernon is extraordinary. He knows everyone it seems and everyone knows him. He'd been in the company at Colchester when I was sixteen, when he was fresh from University. During the two plays I did at Colchester, I had my seventeenth birthday. I still have a lovely book on modern art that Vernon gave me at that time. I was going to remind Vernon of our time at Colchester but of course, he remembered perfectly, and, indeed, brought programmes and photos to the theatre one day of the productions we'd done together all those years before.

It was indirectly through Vernon that I met the star of the opening play of our Chichester season: *Waters of the Moon* by RC Sherriff, a play I was not in.

One day I was at the stage door collecting my mail. Suddenly, I turned round, and saw this tall woman wearing a raincoat and a headscarf. She had a rather lined face but the most beautiful eyes. When she spoke her voice was lovely – deep and with a slight accent.

She fixed those wonderful onto me.

"Do you know Vernon Dobtcheff?" she asked me.

I told her that yes, I did. He was in *Caesar* with me.

"He came last night to see the play I am in. He left me a charming note. Would you tell him that I received it and thank him for me and tell him I will reply to it very soon?"

I said that of course I would. She didn't need to tell me her name. I had just had a close encounter with Ingrid Bergman. Thanks to Vernon!

One young actor in the company was living in a cottage outside Chichester. I, being a non-driver, was living in the city centre. This actor invited some of us for dinner one Sunday during our run. Because of the logistics of getting there, I turned down the invitation. Those who went told me what a treat I'd missed. The food was wonderful, apparently. And so were the wines that were served. This actor eventually swapped performing onstage for an altogether different role on television as an expert on wine. The actor's name was (and still is) Oz Clarke.

Keith Michell, as well as running the company, directed a play that season, wrote part of another, designed a production and the season's programmes. You'd think that he'd have had enough on his plate. But Keith cast himself as King Magnus in Shaw's *The Apple Cart*, which was directed by Patrick Garland and was the last play of the season. Famously, King Magnus has one of the longest speeches in any play. It goes on for pages and actors who play Magnus often get a round of applause at the end of the speech, not so much because they were good, but because they got through it. Keith got his round of applause every night but he never really knew it.

The production, which also starred Penelope Keith, was to transfer from Chichester to the West End. You'd think, therefore, that Keith would rest on his laurels and have a break to prepare for the West End transfer. But no. He decided to play Thomas à Becket in TS Eliot's *Murder in the Cathedral*, that was to be performed in Chichester's magnificent cathedral. Some of us stayed on to do it.

It was to be done as a promenade performance (Patrick Garland again directing) so that the audience moved around the cathedral following the action. I had a scene with Keith (I played a young priest), and it was terrifying because he was pretty wobbly on his lines and I knew that if he 'dried', I would not be able to help. Improvising in verse was not one of my skills.

I was very fond of Keith. He was an exciting actor as he proved as Henry VIII for the BBC in *The Six Wives of Henry VIII*. And he had a lovely warm singing voice too as he showed in *Robert and Elizabeth* (the Ron Grainer/Ronald Millar musical about the romance between Robert Browning and Elizabeth Barrett). I loved that show. Keith was splendidly dashing as Browning and June Bronhill sang ravishingly as Elizabeth.

Ah, June Bronhill! I adored June. I got to know her well. My nickname with some of my friends is 'Gordy'. It was June who first called me that.

Her voice was glorious. I am sure most people know the story of her growing up in Broken Hill in a remote part of Australia. The town encouraged her singing and supported her financially so that she was able to come to London to train and work. Her way of saying 'thank you' was to change her surname from Gough to Bronhill (a contraction of Broken Hill).

June shone in operetta and was a stalwart of the Sadler's Wells opera. When the opera company moved to the Coliseum Theatre and changed its name to the English National Opera, June was expecting to get the call to go and sing something with the company. The call didn't come.

However, the company mounted a production of *The Merry Widow,* which was to tour the UK, and it did have one performance at the Coly with June as the eponymous widow. I was there with Tony, one of June's closest friends, and we had VIP seats in the front row of the Dress Circle.

The theatre was packed with June's fans. They didn't want to miss her one and only appearance at the Coliseum. I had never seen so many people standing in the aisles.

When June first appeared, the audience just went crazy. The show stopped. She had to indicate to the audience to cease their cheering so the show could continue. When she sang the famous aria *Vilja*, you could feel that June was in her element. That song, this operetta, that role, this theatre. At the end, the roar was deafening and the cheering prolonged. She had no choice but to sing it again. I think she sang it a third time before she turned to the audience and said, "I'll have to get on or we'll be here all night."

The fans yelled back, "We want to be here all night!"

The curtain call was a triumph. Tony and I headed backstage but it was so crowded, we went off for a drink and returned later. It was still pretty busy, but eventually we made it to June's dressing room which was packed with friends and fans alike knocking back the champagne.

There was a party being held in her honour in Knightsbridge, to which Tony and I were invited so, eventually, about an-hour-and-a-half after the end of the show, we bundled into the huge car with June, Tony and me in the back surrounded by enough flowers and plants to fill an averaged sized garden-centre.

I remember nothing about the party except that I met and talked to Olive Gilbert. When I tell this story nowadays, I am met with, "Who?" so I'll explain. Olive Gilbert was a contralto/mezzo soprano who created many leading roles in Ivor Novello's most famous musical shows. If you'd ever heard her voice, you'd not forget it.

Around 3:30 I decided it was time I went home. It had been a thrilling evening.

June was still being the 'life and soul' of the party when I found her and said that I was heading home.

June decided that she too would go. She had to get up early the next morning to get to Manchester where *The Merry Widow* was to have its second performance.

She asked how I was going to get home. I told her I'd grab a taxi. "No," she insisted. "We'll take you home in the car."

"But, June, you live around the corner from here. I'm in West Hampstead."

She had decided. And when June decided something, you went along with it. We again bundled into the huge car. The long-suffering driver set off for West Hampstead and my flat.

When we arrived, June said, "What about all these bouquets and flowers? I am off to Manchester tomorrow. I can't take them with me. You have them."

I protested but it was to no avail. With the driver's help and making a lot of journeys up the stairs to my top floor flat, we carried the flowers. The smell was heady. For over a week, I lived in a garden!

The last time I saw June was when she played the Abbess in a revival of *The Sound of Music* with Petula Clark as Maria. June had herself played Maria in the original Australian production years before and must be the only actress/singer to have sung both roles.

She hung on in London but there wasn't enough work for her, so she returned to Australia where, of course, they welcomed her with open arms. Her final years were rather sad but her career was a tremendous one. Every time I hear her singing *Climb Every Mountain*, I admit that the tears never fail to come.

Keith Michell came into London with *The Apple Cart,* as did Penelope Keith. I didn't work with Penny, although a few years later, a friend of mine, Janet, worked on a stage play she was in. It was summer and Penny invited the cast and crew to her beautiful house near Guildford for a garden party. Janet asked me to join her. The garden was magnificent and as it was summer it should have been perfect. However, typically, the Sunday of Penny's garden party turned out to be very cold indeed. We were ushered into the garden and if we dared to creep back into the house to warm up, we were told by Ms Keith, "No, no. Out you go. It's a garden party!"

Actually, she was a delightful hostess and I did manage to spend time indoors talking to her in her magnificent sitting room although my abiding image of the party was Belinda Carroll disconsolately playing tennis in what looked like a fur coat.

Years later BBC Radio 4 made a documentary about *Mrs Dales' Diary/The Dales* and the producer had assembled a group of us who were involved in that popular radio soap: producers, studio managers and, of course, any actors who were still around. I was one who was and I was duly interviewed by the presenter, who was none other than Penelope Keith, a huge fan of the series!

The first job I did after Chichester was *When the Boat Comes in* on television. In fact, I did quite a few Geordie parts around that time. The first 'Geordie' part I played was in the Robert Louis Stevenson serial *St Ives*. This was long before anyone outside of Newcastle knew what a Geordie accent was. I remember the director asking me to tone down the accent so that viewers would understand what I was saying. How different it was later (after people had got used to the accent, especially in series like *When the Boat Comes in*) when I was acting in the classic Sid Chaplin/Alan Plater musical play, *Close the Coalhouse Door*, for the BBC World Service. In a comparatively short time, the Geordie accent became recognised and Gordon House (the producer of *Coalhouse Door*) gave me a note to say that I could 'go even stronger' on the accent! James Bolam who starred in *When the Boat Comes in* was also the star of *Close the Coalhouse Door*.

I was particularly pleased to have a scene with James Garbutt in *When the Boat Comes in* because my very first appearance as a thirteen-year-old at the Rep in Tynemouth was in a comedy by Ian Hay called *Housemaster* and the eponymous housemaster was played by Jimmy Garbutt in his first leading role after having given up his job as a teacher.

I also played Andy's dad, Tom, a pitman struggling to bring up his family in *Andy Robson*, a Tyne-Tees serial.

So I divided my time, certainly in television, between playing gritty Geordies as well as doctors, policeman and a lot of clergyman. I kept being told I looked like a vicar which I always thought a bit odd. Some vicars look like bouncers and vice-versa.

As I mentioned previously, I was totally bilingual: Geordie and non-Geordie. I spoke (and still do) with what was then called a 'BBC voice', my voice was RP (received pronunciation). I had 'no accent' but I discovered that that was no longer the case when I was cast as another priest in a mini-series version of Rosamunde Pilcher's wartime novel *Coming Home* that starred Peter O'Toole and Joanna Lumley.

Now, here's a coincidence. I was showing my very good Catalan friend, Jordi, around the UK. We spent a long weekend in Cornwall based in St Ives. One day, after a long walk along the beach, we decided to get the little train that runs to St Ives from Penzance. We weren't quite sure where the nearest station was but we came off the beach to look for it. Ahead of us on a slight rise was a beautiful church surrounded by a churchyard full of what seemed like very old gravestones. I just had to have a look inside. It was very calm and peaceful and still.

Less than two months later, I went to meet the director of *Coming Home*, Giles Foster and he cast me (with the help of my friend, Allan Foenander, the casting director) as… a priest, a family friend of Colonel Cary-Lewis (O'Toole) who has a scene where he conducts the funeral service for the Colonel's wife. It was to be based in St Ives and the church where we filmed my scenes? Amazingly, it was the one I'd discovered while out for a walk with Jordi just a few weeks before!

Peter O'Toole was very naughty. After I'd done my scene in the church, saying what a lovely woman his late wife was, I had to stand outside the church facing the camera and O'Toole, with his back to me, was supposed to be saying something like, 'Thank you for a lovely service, Vicar'. There was no sound for this sequence, thank goodness, because what O'Toole said to me (with a twinkle in his eye) was something unrepeatable here.

While there was a break in filming, the stars would escape to their canvas chairs in a quiet area slightly away from the church and the extras. The extras were dressed in wartime clothes and there were a lot of them. A whole congregation full! One came up to me and asked if I minded a crew filming in my church! I explained that I was not a priest but an actor. Without anything better to do than hang around, quite a few latched on to me and one actually asked me to tell her the history of the church!

Dear Joanna Lumley! She noticed that I was being mobbed and she came over and said, "Oh, Gordon, would you join us for a moment?" She led me over to where O'Toole and the others were resting. "I thought perhaps you needed a break," she said, indicating a free chair.

There was a dialogue-coach attached to the company. At first I thought this rather odd. None of the characters had significant accents, so why a dialogue-coach? Then I discovered that the dialogue-coach was for the young members of the cast (which included a very young Keira Knightly and Paul Bettany in one of his first starring roles). The dialogue-coach had to make sure they didn't sound 'modern'. So, my voice, which had been described as 'accentless' was now an accent. Because it was a period piece, the young actors had to be monitored to make sure they retained what had once been regarded as 'received pronunciation'. It seemed it wasn't 'received' anymore!

Being able to speak in a Geordie dialect had its advantages but it also had disadvantages too. I'd go for a Geordie role and the directors would invariably say, 'But you don't sound like a Geordie' and I'd have to go through the whole story again about how I had got rid of my accent because, in those early days, any 'accent' was limiting. If they let me read something from the script, I was able to convince them that the accent was indeed authentic and I didn't have to 'put it on'. That way I usually was given the part.

The fish quay at North Shields was a very familiar place to me as a boy growing up in the northeast. During the school holidays I'd sometimes get up early and go with my dad to the fish quay where he'd buy his fish for the day.

The fish quay was an exciting place with the boats lined up and the buzz and activity as the fish merchants bargained and bought their supplies. The smell was of the sea and of the fumes from the smoke houses. And, of course, of fish. I know most people don't like the smell of fish but I love it. It's a smell from my childhood. Another thing I remember of the quay was the deafening cries of the seagulls hovering, waiting to pounce. After I'd helped my dad stack the containers with his purchases into the back of his van, we'd drive to his shop in Byker and unload it.

So I knew the fish quay well. Everyone who worked there knew my dad and my dad knew everyone who worked there. One of the characters on the quay was Tom Hadaway who later became a writer and wrote of his experiences as a 'fish' man. I had received word that the BBC were going to do one of Hadaway's plays so I pleaded with my agent to get me an interview for it.

The producer and director interviewed me at The Rex Hotel in Whitley Bay. The Rex was once a very grand hotel where stars who were appearing in Newcastle would stay, or footballers playing at St James' Park. As a kid, I would often wait outside the front of the hotel to get the autographs of Frankie Vaughan or Tommy Steele. Now the hotel is closed. I stayed there when I was giving some talks in the northeast a couple of years ago. It was a sad experience. Threadbare carpets, old dark bedroom furniture. It seemed empty and faded. The magic had gone.

I went in to see the director and producer of this television play, and, of course, I was told I didn't sound Geordie, so yet again I told my story and also how the fish quay was such a part of my life. I asked if I could read for them. They said no, I didn't get the part. Maybe there was someone better available. And to play the part you didn't need to have known the fish quay but (if you'll pardon the pun) I was gutted!

I do think some directors have little imagination. I repeat, some. Most are friendly and helpful (I have to say that, just in case…), but an example of a director without much imagination:

Not long after I left Sheffield and I was back in London, I got a call from the BBC to go and see a well-known director. Anne Stallybrass had been cast in a play and she'd recommended me for a part in it: a disruptive teenager. The director told me that Anne was full of praise for my work which was very good to hear. We chatted in a friendly way and for a while I thought, *Well, that's it. The part is mine.* The director was talking as though I were going to play it. Then he leaned forward to fill in a form on his desk.

He said: "Sorry about this but I just need to get some information down here." And he took my name, address and telephone number and then asked for my agent's details. Then he said, "And how old are you?"

"I'm twenty-two," I told him.

He put down his pen, leaned back in his chair, looking sad.

"Oh, what a pity," he said. "This character you're up for is eighteen!"

I didn't get the part!

Another director asked me what kind of actor I was. I didn't know what he meant so I asked him to explain.

"I mean; how would you describe yourself in an 'acting' context?"

I felt like saying, "I am a 5'11, fair, blue-eyed type of actor," but just looked rather blank.

He was getting a bit annoyed. "I just want you to say what kind of actor you are? Comic, dramatic, Shakespearean…"

"Well, yes. All of those. I am an actor. I have done a lot of comedy. I have played a lot of dramatic roles. I have done Shakespeare and Feydeau farce and restoration comedy."

He tried another tack. "If I asked you what part would you like to play, what would be your response?"

"Whatever part you think I'd be suitable for, I will play." I didn't get the part!

I was kept busy with television and theatre and I was popping back to do radio work from time to time too. I was also doing voice-over work. Narration for documentaries. That sort of thing.

As I mentioned before, when I left drama school there was no 'talking books' industry. But with the emergence of cassettes, a couple of companies started recording books onto cassette. I thought this was something that I could do.

I went to my local library in Swiss Cottage, North London and went to the small section that dealt with this new concept. I randomly pulled out a nicely produced package which contained the cassettes of an 'audiobook' (although that term wasn't yet used) and my intention was to jot down the address and telephone number of the company that was producing the book so that I could write to them and send an audition cassette or at least try to get an interview.

When I turned the package over, I received a shock! The company – called Soundings – was based in Whitley Bay! My hometown! That didn't seem possible.

But the next time I went to see my mum, who by now had a flat in the centre of Whitley Bay, I arranged to see the boss of the company.

We had a pleasant chat, he was impressed with my experience and he offered me not one book to record, but four!

Little did I know where those four books would lead!

Part Two
Being There

Chapter 13

As I said before, when I left Rose Bruford's I couldn't have predicted that I would make my living recording books. Then, in 1963, there was no such industry. Of course, there were devices to listen to books provided by the RNIB but otherwise, if you'd wanted to listen to, say, *Great Expectations*, you'd have had to buy a lot of LPs. It was just not commercially viable. But now, in the early 1970s, cassettes were being developed and suddenly here was a simple and efficient way to tell stories.

The reader would record the stories on both sides of the cassette, with each side having about 45 minutes' worth of recording time. An average-sized book would only require six to eight cassettes. In the late 1970s, the Sony Walkman was introduced and suddenly one could listen to music on the move: in the street, on the train, in bed!

In Whitley Bay, the northeast town where I'd spent most of my childhood, the public library was already providing music on cassette but decided it might be a good idea to put stories onto cassette too. But who could provide them?

At that point there was only one company that I can recall doing this work. It was very early days. The library had, of course, long provided LP albums alongside books, and the special music albums were provided by Derek and Stella Jones who ran a specialist record shop in Park View in Whitley Bay.

Derek was passionate about big band music and singers like Lena Horne, Doris Day and Sinatra. Stella supplied country and western records. One day, the librarian went to see Derek and Stella, and asked if they would be able to provide stories on cassettes – in effect, 'talking books'.

It was something that Derek had not thought about. But the more he did think about it, the more he thought that it was viable. He, at that time, had no recording studio and knew no actors or indeed anyone who could read for him. He knew that he'd have to find not only readers but also studios.

When I went to see him, he'd not recorded many books and generally had used local actors but when he heard that I had a lot of experience in radio, he entrusted me with four books. His company (one of the first in the UK) was called Soundings (a neat punning name because Derek had been a navy man).

As Soundings didn't have their own studio, my first books were recorded in a studio attached to a house in the Northumbrian village of Haydon Bridge. A very experienced sound-recordist lived there with his wife and little girl. The plan was that Derek would drive me to Haydon Bridge on a Friday afternoon, leave me with the family and collect me on the Monday or Tuesday when the book had been recorded.

It worked well. I was royally looked after and before I started work, there'd be a splendid Friday night meal *en-famille*. The daughter was a huge fan of the Channel 4 show I did for small children called *Chips' Comic* in which I played the amiable odd-job man, Inky. I'd recorded the songs from the show and was able to give her a copy so that I became her friend for life!

I was up early on the Saturday morning to start recording my very first audiobook.

I was in a room on my own and my producer was in another room where he had his equipment. We did a brief sound-check and I started to record my first book.

It was all going very well when, suddenly, there was the most tremendous banging noise that terrified the life out of me. "What's that?" I asked into the microphone.

The embarrassed reply came: "Oh, I am so sorry. I should have warned you. That's the central-heating coming on. Let's give it a few minutes and the noise will stop." We gave it a few minutes and the noise did indeed stop. I continued with the dramatic story. This was my first audiobook and it was going so smoothly. After about ten pages or so, I heard a 'ding dong' and stopped recording. The voice said, by way of explanation, "Oh, sorry, Gordon. That'll be the milkman. I need to pay him. Won't be a minute."

And that's how it was for the rest of the recording. The equipment was state-of-the-art and the recording sounded great. The problem was that the room I was in wasn't soundproofed.

Some months ago, I came across the recording of that audiobook and, curious to hear what it sounded like, I played it. It wasn't bad at all. It concerned gun smuggling off the coast of Uruguay and in one very dramatic scene on a boat near Montevideo, a dodgy gang were whispering conspiratorially. They planned to kill the captain of the boat. The dramatic whispering continues as they decide who shall do the dastardly deed and then, if you listen very carefully, you can hear a Northumbrian cow mooing in the background!

Often, after one of my talks about my life in audiobooks, someone will come up to me and say that they'd like to do what I do. They've been told that they have a nice voice and they think they'd be right to record audiobooks. The first question I ask is, "Have you a good ear?" (Well, two good ears for preference). But seriously, if you want to record audiobooks it's obvious that a 'nice voice' is not enough. You need to be able to do a variety of accents and voices. My first four books for Soundings were a rollicking tale of gun-smuggling in and around Montevideo, a romantic saga set in the north of Scotland, an exciting story of kidnapping and murder in Italy and Malta and a whodunit set in Yorkshire! So, you see, you cannot be fazed by lots of accents or by a variety of styles and myriad characters.

We readers were farmed out to various studios in the north. I spend some happy weeks recording in a studio near Manchester. The set-up was similar to the Northumbrian one. I stayed with the owner of the studio, Steve, and his family. His house adjoined the studio. I'd record all day but after I'd had dinner with the family, Steve took me into the studio to do another hour and a half of recording. No one else was there,

there were no distractions. All was dark except for the light in Steve's recording booth and the angle-poise lamp on my desk. It was at one of these evening sessions that I realised how much I enjoyed recording these books, telling these stories. I was relaxed. I relished telling the tales. I didn't find it difficult at all. I took to it like a duck to water. And I had no problems with my voice.

People often ask how I manage to record from nine until five o'clock, or whatever, without the voice getting croaky or tired. The answer is that I don't know. It just doesn't.

My problem in those early days was not my voice but the back and neck pain I sometimes got. But that was easily sorted. I had to find a position to sit in that was comfortable. A position that allowed me to sit up (not slouch) and be relaxed and comfortable, just as I would be if I were at home in a comfortable armchair reading a story to friends or family. The only difference being that, while recording, I had to sit perfectly still, making sure my head didn't ever turn away from the microphone. As someone who waves his arms around when he talks, it took me a while to learn how not to do that.

It was at these Manchester studios that I recorded my first Catherine Cookson novel. I knew that Mrs Cookson (she was not yet a Dame) was very particular about who recorded her books. I knew that she listened punctiliously to all the recordings and wasn't averse to giving notes. My recording of *The Long Corridor* was published so I assumed it had passed muster.

I went on to record all the Catherine Cookson novels that had a male narrator (*The Man Who Cried*, *The Gambling Man*, etc.). It was after recording her novel, *The Upstart,* that I received my first letter from her. She was by now frail and bedridden but still feisty and still working. Thank goodness the letter praised my reading.

The story told of a cobbler who, from humble beginnings, had done well for himself. He was able to buy a rather grand house but with the house, he'd inherited the rather snooty butler. The butler regarded the cobbler as an 'upstart' – hence the title of the book. The letter from Dame Catherine (yes, by now she was a Dame) was pages long and she clearly recognised that I was (like her) from the northeast. We all had pretentions to be someone other than we were, she proclaimed. We were all upstarts!

I knew that Dame Catherine had a chip on her shoulder about her very humble beginnings but one would have thought that her massive success as a writer would have satisfied her. But no. We were all 'upstarts'. She and (by implication) me.

She wrote more letters to me and I found them rather sad. All that success and she still seemed not to be satisfied. Her headed notepaper had at the top 'Dame Catherine Cookson', followed by all the other honours and doctorates she had been given. Obviously, she wanted to show what she'd achieved. But it clearly wasn't enough.

Cookson's books were fun to record because, although she wasn't a brilliant writer, she was a superb storyteller. I particular relished the characters with very strong Geordie accents. The Catalan mother of a friend of mine was an avid reader. Her favourite writer was Catherine Cookson. She read as many of her books as she could get hold of. In Spanish or Catalan, presumably. Dame Catherine may not have been accepted by 'the gentry' (a favourite phrase of hers) but for a working-class girl from the middens of South Shields, she hadn't done too badly.

Eventually, Derek, the boss of Soundings, found a small house, that had also been a jeweller's, in Whitley Bay. This became the headquarters of the emerging company. Downstairs was the office and reception, and upstairs, the studio. It was well-equipped but books still had to be farmed out to other studios because the Soundings building only had one studio so could only record one or two books a week. It meant that often books were recorded at weekends as well as during the week.

I was there recording a book called *The Lantern Network* by Ted Allbeury, a favourite writer of Derek's. It was the weekend. There was just me, Derek and the engineer. It was an exciting book and I could see that Derek was in his element.

He often told me that that weekend made him realise that this was the work he wanted to do. He wanted to make Soundings an important company. To record books. But he knew even then, that the converted shop was not going to be big enough.

This was all great for me. I was having fun telling stories. I was in regular work recording at least two books a month and I was getting some smashers. I recorded *A Tale of Two Cities* fairly early on and it led to my first review in *AudioFile* magazine in the US. Not only was it a wonderful review (paraphrasing the opening of the book, the reviewer called it 'the best of reads'. I couldn't have written better myself!) but the magazine gave me my first Golden Earphone award for it. So, I must have been doing something right. I was more pleased for Soundings than I was for myself.

So, twice a month, I would zip up from my home in London to the Soundings studios. Other readers stayed in a nearby hotel, I stayed with my mum. She was thrilled. I'd arrive home after a long studio day and there was a table beautifully laid out for my dinner. Delicious smells would be coming from the kitchen. No sooner had I got in than I was ushered to the table and fed. Royally. It was a bit early for me to eat but old northern habits die hard. We all gained from it, though. My widowed mum had something to do and, of course, I had some delicious home cooking.

It soon became clear that the small studio we were recording in was too small. Two studios at least were needed as the company got bigger. But move where?

The centre of Whitley Bay is dominated by St Paul's Church which has played a significant part in my life. My parents were married there and my brother Andrew and I were in the church choir. We were confirmed there too and in 2001, as blossom drifted from the churchyard trees, my mother's funeral service took place there.

St Paul's Church hall was a splendid red-bricked building, not more than five minutes' walk from the church. After Sunday's family communion service, there was tea and chat in the church hall. But it was eventually decided that a more up-to-date hall should be build next to the church – more modern with better facilities. And that's what happened. So, the old church hall was now redundant and the lease was up for sale. Derek made a bid for the premises and eventually St Paul's Church Hall became the headquarters of Soundings. On the premises, books were recorded and then duplicated, packaged, labelled and distributed. There were spacious offices and a kitchen and workroom as well as the two fully equipped studios.

I remember the excitement of recording my first book there, *Spella Ho* by H E Bates. It was a double excitement because by an extraordinary coincidence, my very first appearance on any stage (as I mentioned earlier) as a King in a Nativity Play when I was eight or nine, was on the stage of this very building. Thirty years later, I was back.

When I recorded my fiftieth book, there was much celebrating. No one had recorded fifty books before, as far as we knew, so it was a sort of landmark for Soundings and, of course, for me. I recall that the book was Michael Dobbs' excellent novel set in Berlin (*Wall Games*). All the staff got together during a lunch break and there was champagne and a cake in the shape of a book which may or may not have had fifty candles on it. I was a bit concerned that I had to go back into the studio with two or three glasses of fizz in my bloodstream. But I needn't have worried. I sailed through the afternoon session!

When I recorded my hundredth book, I remember wondering whether there'd be more champagne, more celebrations. I was walking towards the studio and Derek, the boss, was heading towards me. "Ah, Gordon," he said. "I believe it's your hundredth recording today, isn't it?" I admitted, with an embarrassed smile, that it was. "Well done!" he said and walked on!

The company was taking off. Audiobooks were taking off. No time for champagne. Back to work!

Chapter 14

There were still few companies recording books. Derek regarded them as 'the competition'. One of these companies approached me about recorded a book for them. I asked Derek what he thought. He said, "It's up to you, lad, but I'd rather you didn't." And of course I didn't. They then asked if I'd at least produce for them. That was acceptable and I produced a handful of books notably a couple of John Higgins books with that fine actor Stephen Rea. I also produced Tarquin Olivier recording *My Father Laurence Olivier.*

But I wasn't just recording and producing books. I was doing quite a bit of television work and a lot of radio. I was missing the theatre. I said to anyone who'd listen: "I want a nice juicy theatre role. I don't care where. As long as it's a part I can get my teeth into."

I love to travel. Anywhere. And always thought it would be exciting to combine my work with travel. After all, friends were filming in Hungary or touring Africa, or even filming a commercial in the South of France. But it never happened to me, unless you count a week in Luxemburg and Brussels with the Chichester Theatre Company in 1977. Or a commercial for Peter Stuyvesant cigarettes that I filmed in Munich (no, I have never smoked). So the idea of doing a play at the English Theatre of Hamburg appealed.

The company was formed in 1976 by a group of (mostly) Americans who found themselves in Hamburg (mostly teaching English). Two of the group had been professional actors and so, inevitably, they decided to put on plays in English. These productions became very popular so that they eventually searched for a theatre that would become a permanent home where they could perform plays regularly. In

English. There are so many people in Germany and particularly (it seems) in Hamburg, who speak English but would they be able to have a permanent company and run a profession theatre?

They worked hard, day and night, converting a beautiful art-deco swimming baths into a theatre. They chose their opening plays and, initially, played the parts themselves. Word got round and the audiences started to come. They were ambitious and the future plan was to perform plays in English with all the cast being made up of professional actors. That meant recruiting from London. The directors had to hire a flat in London that had enough room for the auditions. As I waited for my audition, I had had to hover on the staircase outside the flat. There wasn't enough room inside.

The play they were casting was *Mr Fothergill's Murder* by Peter O'Donnell, a thriller. O'Donnell had created the hugely successful comic strip, *Modesty Blaise,* but this was a rare venture into writing plays.

The main character is a writer of children's books who is eventually 'taken over' by one of his creations (Mr Fothergill). When the writer discovers his wife is having an affair, he plans to kill the wife and the lover (with the help of the sinister Mr F). Shakespeare it wasn't but I was auditioning for the part of the writer and that was a wonderful part. Lots of light comedy at the beginning but by the end, when he is slowly going mad, it's quite a challenge for any actor. He's onstage for the final chunk of the play on his own. Just him. The actor playing this part had to be good. He had to carry the play. I knew I wanted to play it.

After a series of auditions I was offered the role. The director told me later that they knew that they wanted me from the first time I auditioned but I still had to go back three more times. When eventually I got the call, I was just about to head off to Soundings to record a book which I'd complete on Friday evening. The cast was being flown out to Hamburg for the four-month season on the Sunday. That gave me just over twenty-four hours to pack and rearrange my life for my long absence from London.

I had a wonderful time in Hamburg. I was there over the winter period and it was very cold, very wet and it snowed a lot.

Hamburg was badly bombed during the war so the centre is mostly very modern but the effect of downtown Hamburg is stunning as the city is built around the massive Alster Lake. There are lakes and canals and 2,500 bridges, more than London, Venice and Amsterdam put together. In previous winters, the lake had frozen over so that one could walk on the ice, and stalls were set up selling glühwein and würst. Sadly, it wasn't cold enough for that when I was there.

I shared a small but warm apartment with Peter Joyce, who played my wife's lover in the play and after the show we'd go for a drink at a bar near our flat. As soon as people heard us speaking English, they'd come and chat. They were so friendly. It's so shaming, isn't it, that a German city can run a successful theatre doing plays in English (including the classics of Shakespeare and Shaw and Wilde) for an enthusiastic German audience? It's hard to think of a German Theatre of London doing plays in German for the delight of English audiences.

Peter and I were in the bar having a late-night drink. I happen to mention to him, as the clock passed midnight, that it was my birthday. A few minutes later, a waiter appeared at our table with a large bottle of sekt (Germany's answer to champagne). I explained that we'd not ordered any wine. He said that someone had heard me say it was my birthday and they had ordered the wine. That's the sort of thing that happened. Lovely people.

There were lots of parties (we were there over the Christmas and New Year period) and although the play was demanding and exhausting, I had a wonderful time and got to know Hamburg well.

And it was while I was in Hamburg that I developed my 'no nerves' policy. I had often suffered from nerves when doing a show. This is perfectly normal and many of the biggest names in the theatre have stories about how they would be so nervous before a performance that they'd vomit in the wings before going on. I realised that this wasn't going to work for me.

I remember standing in the wings before the first public performance of *Fothergill.* I was actually shaking with nerves. I gave myself a quick talking to. I had rehearsed to get to this point. I was ready to put into practice what I had rehearsed and I knew that if I was nervous, I wouldn't give of my best.

I remember consciously thinking, "OK. This is it. Calm down. And give the audience what you have prepared. And enjoy it!"

It worked. I am not a fan of 'nerves'. I know most actors will say they like to feel a bit nervous before they go on. I don't. If I am relaxed, I will perform better. If anything goes wrong then I am in control. And this method has worked for me since. As long as I can rehearse and practise and work out what I am doing, then I am happy to present that to the audience whether it's 2000 people in a theatre or a congregation at a memorial service or even giving a Best Man speech at a wedding.

At the end of the book I will tell you when I was really nervous. My excuse was that, in that instance, I had had no rehearsal at all!

Little did I know that as I boarded the plane back to the UK after the run, that I would be seeing Hamburg again. And often.

I had a couple of books to record when I returned to the UK and then back to London to re-adjust to being back home. Then I got a message from the English Theatre directors (this was pre the Internet so I guess it must have been by post. Or maybe a phone call).

The company previously had performed a children's play that helped German children learn English. It had been a success but setting up the production had proved time-consuming (liaising with schools, organising bookings etc.) but they wanted to have another go. Robert Rumpf, one of theatre's co-founders, had written the play and needed a bunch of English actors to be in it. They were very busy with their evening performances and didn't have time to come to the UK to cast it. Would I cast it for them? I was amazed at this unexpected request but I thought: *Why not?* I knew a lot of actors; I'd been around a long time so I said yes. I advertised and sent out a breakdown with my requirements, set up auditions and eventually chose my cast.

Rather nervously I sent the actors off to Hamburg. By luck or by judgment, they were a lovely bunch. Not only were they very good actors but they all got along well and had a great time. That pleased me, of course. The directors invited me to the English Theatre to see the performance. They were paying my flight so I said that I'd be delighted to come.

Whilst I was there, I was called in to a meeting with Robert and co-director, Clifford Dean. They had a proposal for me. Would I be their permanent casting-director? It would mean casting four plays a year. They would send out the breakdown but the actors, rather than writing to Hamburg with their CVs, would write to me. I'd do initial auditions and then select the best for recalls. The director would come to London for the recalls and choose the final cast.

And so began my long and very happy and successful association with the theatre. I have cast countless plays from Shakespeare to Tennessee Williams, from Ayckbourn to Wilde, from farce to musicals. Nowadays, with the Internet, everything is so much easier. In fact, the directors don't any longer come for the recalls. I film the recalls and they can sit at home in comfort and watch the auditions before making their final choices. Of course when I am casting with 'outside' directors, then we cast together in London.

I love it when actors who really want the job get it. I also feel the pain of actors who aren't successful. But I think what I bring to the job is a sense of being 'simpatico'. I have myself been to so many auditions where I've been treated not as a professional with a lot of experience but as a commodity. Yes, you're right. No, you're wrong. I was determined that actors who auditioned for me would get respect and time to show what they could do. Sometimes an actor would walk into the audition room and I would know straight away that they were wrong but I can guarantee that the actor would not know that that was what I felt.

I love actors. I love agents too but sometimes they can be trying. There was one actress who had applied many times for Hamburg. At last, I found a part that was right for her comedic skills. It was early December I remember. I gave the details to the agent. The agent got back to me and said that (let's call her 'Sarah') Sarah couldn't make it. I said that I was auditioning all that day and as I knew that she wanted to work at The English Theatre, I could be flexible with the time. The agent promised to get back to me. No, the agent told me, the actress wasn't able to come to the audition. I asked why. "Because the day of your audition is the only day she has to do her Christmas shopping!" Ye gods.

Another actress wanted to do the job but she had a phobia about underground railways. I explained that if she needed to travel by U-Bahn (the underground system in Hamburg) then she almost certainly wouldn't travel underground as the system was mostly over-ground. She got back to say that she also had a fear of escalators. I was able to assure her that unlike in London, all escalators had stairs beside them as an alternative. And there were buses! When she came back with a third problem, I decided that this wasn't going to work out!

One actor insisted on a car to take him from his flat in Hamburg to the theatre. I explained this was Hamburg not Hollywood. Another wanted top billing on the poster. I explained that the posters were already printed and already displayed all over Hamburg and, in any case, would his name really draw the crowds?!

But mostly, actors are lovely and are in the main just happy to be doing the work with a very good company. I have seen a number of productions at Hamburg that could have transferred straight to the West End.

Some people seem to think that because one was playing to a German audience, that one had to speak really slowly. That's not the case, although the German audiences do have difficulty sometimes with very strong dialects. We have to be careful casting *Educating Rita*, for example. Rita's Liverpool accent must be there, of course, but if it's really thick, they won't understand what she's saying.

We always hope that our actors are fit. If an actor gets sick, then it's a problem for the theatre. There are no understudies and so the play has to be cancelled if the actor can't go on. The theatre relies a lot on money taken at the theatre box-office and if performances are missed, it can be a serious financial problem.

But mostly, actors have a good time at the English Theatre. More than once, a couple have met at the English Theatre, fallen in love and got married. It's a sobering thought that I have brought together actors who first met at rehearsals for the English Theatre and are now happily married and often with a family. I call that good casting! Conversely, actors who were married, have come to Hamburg and met someone and fallen in love with them. So marriages are formed and sometimes broken. The latter though is rare. I love to hear that actors, who became close at the English Theatre, remain friends after the job has ended. A charming young actor in one production died not long after he returned to England and the funeral was attended by his own family, of course, but also by his 'Hamburg family'.

I must have auditioned hundreds of actors over the years and although I have a very good memory for names and faces, I obviously can't remember everyone who reads for me. But if someone I don't recognise comes up to me in a bar or at a theatre and says 'hello', then it's probably an actor I have auditioned over the years. They will often say: "Remember, I auditioned for you about six years ago." Well, I have to admit that I don't always recall that particular audition.

I was walking on Hampstead Heath when an attractive woman, who was quite a way ahead of me, turned round and called out loudly, "Gordon!" She was too far ahead of me to see exactly who she was but I waved at her and acknowledged her with a 'Hi'. An actress I'd auditioned presumably. Again she called out, "Gordon!" and from out of the bushes to the left of me leapt a bedraggled looking terrier. He ran towards his mistress who attached a lead to him. Embarrassing. But whoever heard of a dog called Gordon!

Actors in Hamburg can sometimes supplement their income by doing voice-over work. There are a number of companies in Hamburg that, from time-to-time, require English actors to voice various commercials or announcements and a large publishing company called Jumbo Neue Medien records audiobooks. I knew of Jumbo and told an actor who was at the English Theatre to contact them, as he had experience recording books. He went to see a producer there. He was asked how he came to hear of them and he mentioned my name. The next thing I knew was that they were in touch asking me to come and see them when I was next in Hamburg.

I try to see as many plays as I can but time prevents me seeing them all, but the next time I was in Hamburg, I did go to see them. That interview led to me recording a number of audiobooks in English for the company. I also produced a number of English classics for them too.

But I was still very busy in the UK. Books were still coming in and I was very happy to accept them. I had proved my point that I could still act on a stage in a large and demanding part. I was sure that I'd get more opportunities to do more theatre work. But in the meantime, I was back up in the northeast and doing more recordings.

I'd been recording for the company for quite a few years when I was called in to see Derek, the boss, who had an offer that knocked me for six!

Chapter 15

"Come in, son," Derek indicated the chair in front of his desk. "Have a seat." His wife, Stella, was seated beside Derek, behind his large desk. "Now then," he continued. "I have a proposal to put to you. You don't have to answer straight away but can go away and think about it."

Derek had long been talking of taking it easier. He had worked really hard over the years to build up the company from nothing and he was 'getting on'. He didn't want to sell up. The company was still 'his baby' but he was looking for two people to replace him and Stella. He'd be there to guide, to give advice. It would still be his company but he'd have a manager running the company and Stella would be replaced by an office manager/administrator. But Derek's replacement would have control of the running of the organisation and the decision-making. And then, he came out with it: "Would you be interested in the job?" I was completed nonplussed. I hadn't seen that coming at all.

He reiterated that he didn't want an answer now. He realised that I would be completely taken by surprise by the offer. I was astounded.

"All I want to know is whether you are interested. If you are not, then we'll shake hands and end the conversation. No ill feeling. But I'd expect that before making any decision, you'll need to have a big think about things. I realise that if you were to take on the job, it would change your life drastically. You'd have to live up here in the north-east."

I thanked him very much and was stumbling out of the room when he added, "Oh, by the way. You'd get a company car!" A company car? Wow! Only problem was, I didn't drive!

One of the first things I did after that was check the flights to and from Newcastle and London. Then I talked to family and friends. I had had a long and busy career as an actor but was I ready to give up everything and run the company? I felt, in lots of ways, I could do the job. I had bags of energy and knew the industry so well albeit from the inside. I had ideas. The more I thought about it, the more I was taken with the idea. I wasn't in a relationship at the time so I didn't have domestic or personal reasons for saying no. I would keep on my London flat, in case things didn't work out.

One thing that hadn't been discussed was the money. How much was I to be paid. I wouldn't be doing it for the money but if I was going to make such a big change in my life, I'd need to be reimbursed for it.

Every time I mentioned the money to Derek, he'd say that he'd talk to his accountant and call me in to a meeting to discuss my wage.

Days went by, weeks went by and still we didn't have the vital meeting. Derek came to the London Book Fair and I joined him there. He introduced me to publishers and agents and kept saying, "This is Gordon. He's joining the company." I had to tell him that I hadn't yet made that decision. But I know he was impressed by the fact that I got on well with all the people I met there. I enjoy meeting new people whereas Derek felt rather self-conscious. Very much the 'northerner' and out of place in 'that there London'.

Eventually, I got the call to meet the accountants and I was told how much I'd be paid. I had a vague figure in my mind and I wouldn't accept any figure less than that. The money that was on offer was exactly the sum I'd had in my head as being the 'lowest' I would accept.

I went off to make my final decision. It was really difficult but the money was what (during a good year) I was already earning for recording books. I decided, after much soul-searching, to turn down the job. Derek and Stella were clearly disappointed but there were no 'hard feelings'. But what happened when I left the office after turning down their offer was a huge sense of relief. I felt as though a huge weight had been lifted from my shoulders. I'd not realised that I was carrying such a burden. I clearly was.

I was relieved and happy that I could still go on recording for Soundings. I never for one moment regretted my decision and was so thankful that Derek had such confidence in me. It was flattering but, in the end, I felt that I wasn't the man for the job.

Recording audiobooks requires discipline and efficiency. Both these qualities I have and would have been able to put them to good use had I become manager of the company. But in the end, my decision was the right one.

By now, the audiobook industry was changing. When I started, we were told to imagine a little old lady who can't see very well listening to a family saga on her cassette machine while she does her knitting. By 2000 things were changing dramatically. That little old lady was still there and still listening to her recordings but by now, audiobooks were not just for the visually impaired but for everyone. In the US, many young people were listening to the latest books rather than actually reading them. That trend soon came to the UK.

Other companies opened shop. I was being asked to record for them. I was still recording for Soundings but other companies were employing me too. Audiobooks were becoming important, no longer the poor relation of the published book. Audio versions of titles were being brought out at the same time as the hard-backed books. Publishers took an interest in who was recording the books. Suddenly we readers were 'narrators' – the word inherited from the US. I don't like the term very much. Whatever we do, it is not 'narrate' or at least I hope we don't. The dictionary says a narrator is one who recounts the events of a novel. Recount? That doesn't at all describe what we do. 'Reader' is fine. We are storytellers. 'Narrator' sounds rather remote. Describing? Commentating? That's not it at all. Or shouldn't be. It should be more involving than the word suggests. 'Reader' isn't perfect but I much prefer it.

This was an exciting time for those of us who recorded audios. Suddenly, it seemed that almost any book that was published could be recorded. The range was huge. One week I could be recording the new SAS thriller by Chris Ryan and the next, a classical Greek drama for Naxos.

I got a call to book me for a part in Virgil's *Aeneid* starring a favourite actor of mine, Paul Schofield. I was thrilled. But when I arrived at the studio, I learned that Schofield had recorded all his stuff already and I had to record my lines to be slotted in to what the great man had already done. So I didn't get to meet him. I did, however, record a number of classical books for Naxos including Gogol's wonderful, sweeping novel *Dead Souls* and Plato's *Symposium* in which I played Pausanias.

WF Howes is the UK arm of an American company and they set up business in the UK and I recorded (and still do) many books for them. Their books sold to libraries and I was approached by them to ask if I'd be interested in doing a series of talks for them about the preparation of audiobooks, the process of recording and so on. I worked on a talk that was anecdotal and told of my journey from northeast schoolboy to extremely busy audiobook reader.

I loved this experience. I remember starting at the main library in Exeter with some notes and some extracts to read from books I'd recorded. I soon abandoned the notes and talked without them.

We record audiobooks in a vacuum. We don't get an instant response. As an actor in the theatre, I was used to hearing laughter and applause or feel an audience when it's listening. Or not. But when recording books there is no one there (except the producer and/or engineer and they are involved in doing their own particular jobs). So, standing in front of an 'audience' in a library or at a Readers' Day event, was getting back to what I was trained to do. Perform in front of an audience. In this case I was playing myself. I loved it. I chose the extracts with care. One piece was dramatic, one funny, one demonstrated how I do a multi-voiced scene.

I went all over the UK, giving my talk from Dublin to Dumfries, from Guernsey to Gateshead, from Penzance to Pontypridd. Sometimes, the audience was a group sitting round in a circle, at other times, it was a theatre filled to capacity. It didn't matter. I had an audience.

Once in the wilds of Wales, I was being driven to a library in the valleys somewhere. The weather was atrocious. A rainstorm. The car was swishing along country roads in a river of rainwater. I couldn't recall ever having been out in such terrible weather. I couldn't imagine that anyone would leave home in such torrential weather. We phoned ahead to say we might be a little late as we could only drive slowly as visibility was so poor. We arrived, parked the car and even though the journey from the car park to the library was not far, we were completely drenched. Soaked through. I was convinced there'd be no one there but at least we could dry out and get a cup of tea. We walked into the room where the talk was to be held and the room was packed with an eager and enthusiastic group of people who clapped us as we walked in. It was a memorable occasion for us all.

During 'Make a Noise in Library' fortnight, I was doing four or five talks a week, often two a day. Sometimes, I'd stay overnight in a hotel and that was also fun.

I love chatting to the audiences afterwards too. One lady told me that she'd not been out since the death of her husband and the talk had cheered her up. What she actually said was, "I've not had so much fun since my hubby died!" But I understood what she meant!

I am pathologically punctual. I hate being late for anything so I make sure I get to the venue well ahead of time. It often means that I am hanging around but I'd rather that then getting anxious about being late.

I'd been booked for a talk in the refurbished library in Fife – one of the first events after Gordon Brown had re-opened the building. I set off from London really early. I had a train connection at Edinburgh that would take me to Kirkcaldy and I'd be picked up at the final station and taken to the library.

I was well ahead of my schedule. But between Newcastle and Berwick, the train stopped. Five minutes. Ten minutes. Fifteen minutes. The announcements were vague. No one seemed to know what the problem was. Then we knew.

Someone had thrown themselves under the train ahead of us. The police and ambulances were at the scene. We were obviously going to be there some time.

After an hour, I started to panic because I knew, by then, I would be very late getting to Edinburgh. Thank goodness for mobile phones because it was clear I was going to miss my connection to Kirkcaldy. I needed someone to pick me up by car and whisk me to the library which was quite a long way away. The trouble was I didn't know what time I'd get to Edinburgh. I was well and truly stuck! And panicking!

It must have been two hours later when the train pulled away. I was a gibbering wreck! But at least we were on our way. I was met at Edinburgh and I pleaded with the driver to drive as fast as he legally could. It was just possible I might get there in time. Not long out of Edinburgh, he told me he'd not had lunch and he needed to stop off and get a cup of coffee and a sandwich. Did I want anything? No! Please get your sandwich and let's get on!

I arrived at the library at Kirkcaldy, breathless and ten minutes late. But the audience had been forewarned and (bless them) they waited for me. I was so relieved. The talk went well. After it, I was given a lovely cup of tea. What I needed was a stiff drink. The journey back to London couldn't have been smoother!

When I record, I dress comfortably. And the same for the talks. I think I look casually smart. I only wear a suit for more formal occasions. I just feel more relaxed without a tie when I'm giving my talk. I was surprised therefore when at the question and answer session after one particular talk in West Bromwich, an elderly gentleman, who I must admit looked very dapper, asked me, "Do you always look so scruffy?" I was rather shocked as I thought I looked fairly smart if not suited! I was unusually lost for words!

I was giving a talk in a very posh hotel in Manchester. A well-known writer had talked before me. Then the presenter, with a flourish, announced me. I had only just started when there was a strange noise. It was guide dog being violently sick! Suddenly, staff at the hotel in white coveralls and face masks dramatically leapt into the room to clean up the mess. The blind lady whose dog it was, was mortified. I assured her it wasn't a problem. "It couldn't have been something I'd said," I assured her, "as I'd hardly said anything at all!"

At a Reader's Day at the City Hall in Nottingham, those of us giving talks were sharing the smart Mayor's rooms where we were given tea and sandwiches. I was thrilled to be sharing the room with guest speaker, Armistead Maupin, the American writer whose, *Tales from the City* I'd admired in book form and on TV. He was charming. We talked about his contribution to the gay rights movement in San Francisco in the 70s.

After I'd done my talk, I went into the main hall to hear him give his talk and read from the latest in his sequence of books of *Tales of the City*. It was a fascinating talk. He was very much part of the history of the gay movement and talked movingly of his involvement. When he read extracts from his new book, he seemed less assured.

I'd bought a copy of the book and queued afterwards to get him to sign it for me. He duly did and I told him how much I'd enjoyed his talk. He told me that he'd been very nervous reading the extracts from the book, because I was in the audience! It made him conscious that he wasn't a 'proper' reader. Nonsense of course. If a writer can do it, then it's powerful to have them read their own words.

I mentioned earlier that I had recorded some of Chris Ryan's books. Ryan's real life was probably more exciting than any of his books. He was a member of the SAS and did so many brave and (possibly) foolhardy things. He'd decided that he'd like to record his own stories but I was told by an engineer friend that he was so nervous the first time he attempted it that his hands were shaking! Chris Ryan? Nervous?!

I understand from colleagues in New York that the great Stephen King decided that he'd like to record his own books. He'd done a test-read and he'd not been very fluent, so the company got one of their professional readers to record, unbeknown to King, the first chapter or so of the particular book. Then Stephen settled down to record the book. By lunchtime, not many pages had been recorded. The producer asked King how he thought it was going. "Fine," he said. The producer then explained that, at the rate he was recording, it was going to take about a fortnight to get the book completed. King was horrified. "But I can't afford to put aside two whole weeks just to record the book!"

Then the producer asked him to sit and said, "Listen to this." They played to Stephen King what the professional reader had already recorded. It was the same sequence that King had read.

King listened, nodded, smiled and said, "OK. I'll get my coat!"

Of course, writers are often very possessive about their novels. They want to make sure that the reader understands the characters and the tone of the book etc. Sometimes they need to choose the voice that best suits their work. I have given reassurances to writers that if I was entrusted with their books, I would be sensitive to what was required and that I'd do my very best to bring the story to life.

I am often asked what do I do if I get a book I don't like. Well, I am very lucky because in most of the books, although they are chosen for me, I can find something to enjoy. By someone else deciding what I should read, I've got to read some quite amazing books that I would never have picked up myself in the bookshop. But of course, inevitably, I have had to read books that I didn't enjoy. I remember one particular book which had an appalling leading character. I found him odious, pompous and condescending. He had a vacuous girlfriend who was always twittering on about her designer clothes. The writer had created what she thought were charming characters and so I had to make these characters charming too. It wasn't easy. But as I say in my talks, what I feel about a particular book is irrelevant. It's not about me or my tastes. I am there to serve the writer. The writer is always the most important person in the process and no one will ever know what I feel about a book by listening to my recordings. They all get the same preparation. Obviously, I will take more time to prepare, say, the biography of Alan Turing, than a light-hearted hospital romance. But even the hospital romance must sound real.

I once recorded an historical fiction novel that was written in cod-period dialogue. It really was pretty naff. But I gave it my best shot. I was thrilled when the writer sent me a letter stating how happy she was with my recording which had moved her 'deeply'. Job done!

I think it's true to say that we all enjoy being told stories. It goes back to our childhood and most parents know how excited their children get when it's time for their bedtime story.

Some years ago, after a talk in a large public library, I was approached by a local councillor with an interesting proposal. He believed that the 'bedtime-story' was an important time in a child's life. But when the father was in prison then this relationship is severed. This enterprising council had developed a plan whereby prisoners would record stories onto cassette and in this way, the child can listen to the story read by the dad even though he isn't there. A lovely way for the child to connect with the absent father. The proposal was that I would come to the prison two or three times a week and work with the prisoners who wanted to take part in the scheme, to help and advise them so that the final recording would be as good as it could be.

I felt that having the father read was a good idea anyway, whether helped by a professional or not. I was very interested in the proposal but the logistics didn't work. For one thing, I was (and still am) very busy and finding the time would have been difficult and the travel (taking two to three hours) would make it too complicated. I wonder if they pursued their scheme. In other circumstances, I would have been happy to contribute.

The RNIB has been recording books even before the advent of the cassette which made the recording of novels so much easier than the cumbersome equipment that was used previously. It is, of course, a charity, so consequently, the readers don't get a full fee. I felt that, despite that, as I'd recorded a lot of audiobooks, I might be of use to them and in any case, I wouldn't be doing it for the money but to help out. I applied to offer my services.

I received a letter from the Head Office, offering me an audition on a certain date. I happened to be recording on that date so I wrote back and explained that I would be in a studio on the date of the audition. I mentioned that I was, at that time, recording the new Chris Ryan adventure. I also included a list of the books I'd recorded (at that time about 400). I thought that all my experience might suggest that I knew what I was doing and perhaps didn't need to audition. After about four dates that I couldn't do, we eventually were able to coincide with a date. I was sent the scenes I was to read and I duly prepared them.

It wasn't a difficult audition. I read well. I also had to do a piece of sight-reading. There was a page of typed script face down on the desk. When the green light went on, I was to pick it up and read it without even scanning the scene. I did that and, miraculously, I instinctively understood what was happening, the period and the location (eighteenth century London). I even impressed myself.

The lady who'd been overseeing the audition came into the studio. I thought she'd say, "Oh, that was impressive," or some such. But what she did say was: "We will let you know in the next two weeks whether or not you have been successful!" Fair enough. They didn't know me. But I remember thinking how embarrassing it would be if I failed the audition.

Two weeks later I received the letter to say that I had indeed been successful and that they'd be in touch about a 'new narrator workshop' where I'd be shown around the studio so that I could get used to it and that some 'old stagers' might be on hand to give advice. They gave me a couple of dates.

I wrote back to say that I was pleased to have passed the audition but was recording on both the dates they had suggested. I also said that I thought that I could myself be described as an 'old stager' having recorded so many books!

No, they didn't take the hint and I kept receiving dates for the 'workshop', none of which could I do.

Sometime later I bumped into a colleague who had recorded many books at the RNIB and I told him my story. I thought it was quite funny but he was outraged. He said, "Leave it with me!"

A week later I was booked to record my first RNIB novel and it was the start of a very happy association. I have recorded some wonderful books for the organisation and I am still pleased to record for them when I can.

One music studio recognised that audiobooks were the coming thing and so they adapted their studio to accommodate the recording of books. They negotiated a deal with a local publishing company and so began a very successful partnership. It was so successful that another company asked if they could record their books there too. The management wanted to take on the extra work but didn't want the original company to know that they were also recording books for a rival company. To make sure that company number one didn't find out, the narrators were asked to think of a second name to record under when hired to record for the second company!

I had, at this point, recorded a number of books for the original publishing company and if I wanted to record for the second company, I'd need a pseudonym. So, that is how a few books on my list are recorded under the name of Jack Paulin.

Jack Paulin was my mother's brother. By all accounts a brilliant boy who studied the classics and knew Latin and Greek. He got a place at university, the first person from the Durham mining community where he and my mother lived, to do so.

He was shy and very lonely. He'd go for long walks with his dog, Wallace. He had few friends.

One day he was spotted at the local station studying the times of the trains that passed through the village. The next day he was found dead by the railway track. He'd placed his head on the railway line.

He was reclusive and never spoke of his innermost thoughts so no one really knew what went on in his head. He died long before I was born but I would have loved to have known him. It seemed appropriate that I should take the name of my 'bookish', though very sad, uncle.

Most people recognised that having two names was self-defeating. Initially it proved problematic when being paid. Who was my cheque paid out to? So, the idea was dropped. I went back to using my real name.

I worked in many recording studios. Some were better than others. The smart Wardour Street studio where I often work is very posh indeed with marbled loos and state-of-the-art coffee-machines and bowls of fruit and flowers everywhere. There you are likely to be recording on the same day as some very famous fellow-readers. One day I was there and also recording that day in the other studios were Colin Firth, David Tennant and Michael Ball. I was the only one I'd not heard of!

One studio I worked in was not air-conditioned. The walls were padded to deaden the outside noise and the door was also padded and very thick. You had to use all your strength to open and close it. But once you were trapped inside, the sound was certainly deadened but being a very small room, it became very hot.

One summer I was recording in my shorts and T-shirt, it was incredibly hot. I was drenched in sweat.

At one point my producer said over the talkback, "I am hearing a tapping sound. Any idea what it can be?"

"Yes," I replied through gritted teeth. "It's the sweat dropping onto my script!"

I was starting to feel dizzy. I stopped recording.

"I'm sorry," I gasped. "I can't record any more. I can't concentrate in this heat."

Panic. What to do? Someone had an idea. Why not fill a large bowl with ice-cold water and I could sit at the recording desk with my feet in the bowl!

So a bowl was duly brought and I did indeed put my bare feet into the water. I remember thinking, *This is not the glamorous life that I planned for myself!*

It worked for a short while but it was amazing how quickly the water became warm. Luckily, the book I was recording on that day was set in a rainforest! That's what I call method acting!

Similarly, when I first recorded in Hamburg, I was placed in what was no bigger than a broom cupboard. It was summer. It was hot. I sweltered. Trouble was, I was recording *A Christmas Carol* by Charles Dickens describing icicles and snow-covered streets and people shivering and rubbing their hands against the cold. A great test of my acting and reading skills. I must state that later the company acquired wonderful modern studios although we still had to stop when the postman rang the doorbell!

I enjoyed recording in Germany. It was a thrill getting on the U-Bahn (the city's transit system) and going to work in a foreign country. It felt very grown up.

I love the studio atmosphere. I love that it's just me and a microphone, and no one else there. I can really concentrate with (normally) no distractions. I can really become involved in whatever the story is. This can be a bit embarrassing sometimes.

Once I was reading about a dog that dies. If I'd been reading this at home then I'd feel sad I am sure. But somehow, reading it aloud in a studio on my own… well, I had to stop the recording because I was so moved. This happens a lot. I get very emotional. If it's a really sad book, there are a lot of pauses while I regain my composure.

If I'm sailing through a book and making few mistakes and really involved in the telling of the story, I am in my own world. If I do say the wrong words, for example, and don't realise it and the producer has to interrupt, I sometimes jump out of my skin with shock. For the moments that I am involved in the story, I am in another place, if that doesn't sound too fanciful. And the shock of another voice, cutting into that world, can make me jump.

In some studios, we have to stop if an aeroplane flies over. One studio had to negotiate with a local house owner not to use her hover-mover until lunchtime. I was once recording at an evening session. It was November 5th. The noise of fireworks became too much. We abandoned the session. A fiasco and the producer got a rocket!

But let me say here how important producers are. By the time I arrive at the studio I have done my preparation. I am ready to record. So the producer's function is to make sure I don't make any textual errors and to generally be encouraging. They're an important part of the process.

I remember one delightful producer I had at Soundings. She was a real chatterbox and was fun to work with. In fact it was she who encouraged me to write. I had always thought that I could and in 2001 I wrote a novel. My producer was a film buff and one day I went in with what I thought was a very good title for my novel. She said, "No, you can't use that title. It's already been used!" And she named some obscure film I'd not heard of. She made us all laugh but I don't think anyone could have predicted, even her, that she wouldn't just be making us laugh but millions of others on television and onstage. She was (and still is) Sarah Millican.

Day by day, the studio is my little world. I love it. All I need is lots of water and a comfortable chair and I am happy. And good book helps too!

Chapter 16

Being a 'voice' can bring all sorts of surprising work your way. One day, I received a call asking if I'd like to record the announcements for London Transport for the Underground system. We couldn't find a date when I was free. I was tied up with audiobook recordings. Every date that was suggested clashed with my recording schedule. It was shame, I would've liked to have done the job. But it wasn't possible.

I didn't expect to hear any more. But I was very pleased to get a call from the company that was organising the recording. They wanted me. Eventually it was decided we'd record on a Sunday. Rather grandly, a studio was opened up on that day just for me to record the announcements.

I had to record the names of all the underground stations, firstly with a downward inflection and then with an upward, the idea being that all this information would be fed into a computer and used for any announcement. For example:

'Owing to signal failure at Finchley Road (upward inflection), there will be no trains to Wembley Park (upward inflection) and between Wembley Park (upward inflection) and Stanmore (downward inflection)'. You get the idea! It took ages. There are about 270 stations! I also recorded other announcements including 'Mind the Gap, please'. Fame!

My mother was visiting me and we'd decided to go the British Museum. We were just leaving an underground train at Holborn when suddenly a voice, my voice, said, "Mind the Gap, please!" It was the first time I'd heard it. My mum looked rather bewildered as I kept saying to her, "That's me! That's me!" She was looking around confused and by the time she realised what I was telling her, the announcement had ended.

Another surprising 'voice' gig came completely out of the blue. My friend, Gillian, had decided to spend the summer in her father's lovely villa about an hour's drive from Montpellier in the south of France. I was godfather to Gillian's daughter, Clemmie, now a respected television producer, presenter and journalist but then was a little girl learning the violin. Although I am fairly musical I didn't (and still don't!) play the violin. So Gillian phoned the Royal College of Music and asked if there was anyone (student or ex-student) who would like a free summer holiday, all they had to do was spend an hour each day helping Clemmie with her violin lessons.

Enter Paul. He joined us on the holiday. We hit it off straightaway. He had just formed the London Arts Orchestra made up mostly of ex-students from the Royal College and they had sponsorship from a Japanese company and were getting some engagements. He was its conductor.

One evening we sat on the balcony of the villa overlooking the magnificent Pic St-Loup (a hike up that mountain is worth the effort for the stunning views). We talked of musical theatre, of which at that point he knew little (he later was to become one of the West End's top musical directors especially on shows like *The Producers* and *Mary Poppins*) and we talked of classical music, of course. Paul was a fine violinist and played the piano well too. He knew by now what I did for a living and I just casually said to him, "If you ever need a voice…" And left it at that.

The next day we were again sitting admiring the view, a bottle of the local red wine on a table between us.

"Did you mean it last night when you said you'd do something with the orchestra?" he asked me.

I truthfully answered that yes, I had meant it.

The obvious work for a 'voice' to do with an orchestra is Prokofiev's *Peter and the Wolf*. Paul took my contact details and said he'd be in touch when we were both back in London.

He did get in touch. And I did narrate *Peter and the Wolf* with an orchestra. The first rehearsal sitting with the orchestra and hearing Prokofiev's music all around me was thrilling.

The actual script was rather outdated and I slightly modernised it and inserted a couple of modern references and a joke. (Don't tell anyone!).

The performance was at the beautiful church of St John's in Smith Square in Westminster. It was very exciting although I was initially very nervous. I'd not done anything like this before.

I was introduced and came onto the stage to polite applause, score in hand and took my seat. Paul smiled at me encouragingly and nodded, meaning, 'Is everything all right?' I took it as my cue and started to speak. Paul just had time to grab his baton and cue the orchestra. But it all went very well and it was a memorable evening.

Nowadays a lot of voice-over artistes make quite a bit of money from voicing video games. I narrated one many years ago (one of the first) and it was all rather bizarre. And definitely terrifying.

As I mentioned previously, I regretted that at school they didn't teach languages. I have a feeling I'd have had a facility for it. Many years ago I enrolled at an adult education class determined to learn French. I'd already been to Paris a few times and I had a good ear for the sound of it.

The class was made-up mostly of middle-aged ladies who were rather shy about speaking up in class. I wasn't. And neither was a fellow pupil called Tom. We were the teacher's pets because we were very keen and we did our homework and we weren't at all self-conscious about answering questions or reading in class.

After a couple of years (I missed lots of classes because of work) Tom decided he was going to learn Spanish as well as French. I went along with it and again became quite proficient especially with the 'sound' of the language.

One day Tom came with the information that a recording company was looking for English actors who spoke Spanish with an English accent. He thought I should apply.

"But I've not been studying Spanish long enough."

"But your accent is so good," he insisted. Reluctantly, I recorded a short speech from Lesson One of our Spanish textbook. A Spanish boy packing his suitcase as he leaves his home. The dialogue with his mother was very basic. I sent it off to the address Tom provided.

To say that I was astounded when I received a phone call from the producer of the video game to say that they wanted me to narrate it, would be an understatement.

The game was for the South American market and was based on the story of *The Knights of the Round Table*. When the script arrived, I nearly fainted on the spot. There were pages and pages of Spanish dialogue and instruction. I was (as always) working up in Newcastle the week before the recording and so I took my script with me and worked on it day and night, marking the stresses and going over and over the words.

I arrived back home on Friday evening. The recording was to be on Monday afternoon. I frantically phoned my friend, Jo, who was going out with a Spanish guy who lived and worked in London. I asked Jo if I could come to lunch on Sunday and could she invite Alberto too? It was very important.

Alberto listened to me read from the script. He lit another cigarette and smiled. "Your accent is very good. But the stresses are all in the wrong places!"

I spend an hour with him putting even more marks on my script.

Monday came. In the morning someone from the studio phoned to check that everything was OK. I said I'd worked on the script but they did know that I am not really a fluent Spanish speaker, didn't they?

I was assured they wanted someone who spoke Spanish with an English accent but in any case, if I had any doubts or queries, there'd be a Spanish lady at the studio at 1:30 so I could talk to her. The session started at two. That only gave me half-an-hour with the lady.

By the time I met the lady I was seriously nervous. I'd bitten off more than I could chew, I was sure. It didn't help that the lady gave me a lecture on Spanish grammar. I had to stop her and say, "No, please. Just listen to me. I want to make sure I am making sense." But it was no good. I didn't have time to go over my script with her. She kept saying things like, "You must understand that when a past participle is irregular in Spanish…" etc.

At two, I was at the microphone. The green light went on. I began to speak…

It was some sort of miracle. I got to the end of the first page and hadn't been stopped. Should I just carry on?

Eventually, the producer clicked on his talkback button. "It's all going really well. Just what we want. Carry on…"

Chapter 17

It was becoming clear that my recording schedule was making it more and more difficult to take on other work. At this point, it was never my plan to only record books.

In 1989 I'd heard about a television series that was being cast in Newcastle. They were looking for actors who were based in the northeast. I wasn't of course but if I were to get a part in it, I could stay at my mother's in Whitley Bay. As I was going to be in the area, I telephoned the production office and luckily got straight through to the producer and got myself an audition. I was handed a script with three short scenes from the series and went into the reception at BBC Newcastle to look them over.

I had applied for the job because I was Geordie but in fact this character was not a Geordie. He was a designer from London who comes up to the northeast with his wife and daughter. In the script he was called David Warner. I noticed, to my horror that two of the scenes I was to read involved David driving. I don't drive.

I read for the director/producer, Matthew Robinson and he was encouraging. Not only had I read well, he said, but they had already cast the actress who was to play my daughter and there was a similarity in our looks. I was offered the part. I did suggest that David Warner was the name of a well-known actor and so he said, "OK, call him Michael." But I knew I had one more thing to tell Matthew. Could this be a deal-breaker, I wondered?

"I'm thrilled to be offered the part," I enthused. "But I noticed that a couple of those scenes involved me driving and I don't drive." There then followed a very long pause. I was thinking, *I've blown it.*

But eventually he smiled and said, "We haven't cast your wife yet. We'll make sure that she is someone who can drive. All the scenes that involve the 'family' in the car, we will have 'the wife' doing the driving."

I danced out of the studio. I was so happy. I was to play Michael Warner in this new BBC series. Its name? *Byker Grove*!

At that time we didn't know whether the series would be a success. Only one series was scheduled although we hoped there'd be more. One problem the producers anticipated was that kids watching it in, say Penzance or Portsmouth, wouldn't understand the Geordie accents. The great kids that Matthew and company had assembled were cast because of their strong personalities. But would a nationwide audience understand their speech? Matthew knew I was a Geordie, of course, and I became a 'dialogue-coach' for the series. A dialogue-coach in reverse. Nobody wanted to lose the energy of the young cast but if there was a section of dialogue that Matthew didn't understand, I'd work with the young actors to get them to speak clearer without losing either their accent or their vitality.

My own part was pretty dramatic. Michael Warner comes up from London to Newcastle with his wife and daughter. He's hoping the change of scene will bring life back to the failing relationship with his wife, Clare. But Julie (our daughter, played by the lovely Lucy Knowles) hates Newcastle from the start and is very unhappy.

I spoke the very first line in the very first series of *Byker Grove* when I take my daughter, Julie, around the huge MetroCentre, the modern shopping mall not far from Newcastle. I am trying to persuade her that Newcastle is not so different from London. The shops, the clothes, the cafes are the same. Julie is not convinced. She is, eventually, persuaded to go to a youth club, the eponymous *Byker Grove*, to meet other people of her own age. But the kids at the Grove find this 'posh' Londoner stuck-up and she finds the whole experience 'boring'. But over time she makes friends, particularly with Gil, a young tearaway.

In the meantime, Michael's marriage breaks down and Clare decides to go back to London. In a rather telling scene shot near the iconic Tyne Bridge, we tell Julie that her mum is going back to London. Julie shocks her parents by deciding to stay with her dad. By now she's in a relationship with Gil. She doesn't want to leave him.

We knew that I'd stay on if we did a second series and I knew that I'd have some dramatic scenes with me trying to deal with my now-wayward daughter. But as I said, we didn't yet know that we'd do a second series.

I remember one early scene where Michael and Julie arrive home after shopping. I get out of the Volvo estate (no, it wasn't me driving) and unload the shopping and a grumpy Julie gets out too. It was a fairly short sequence and it was filmed at what was supposed to be the exterior of the Warners' house. Not far away was a huge field of rapeseed. I suffer from hay fever and suddenly I started to sneeze violently. Amazingly, Lucy (my daughter, 'Julie') started to sneeze too. We both had an allergic reaction. The make-up people had to keep placing wet chamois leathers on our faces to cool us down between shots. So 'daughter' Julie had inherited her 'dad's' allergic reaction.

Working on Byker Grove was great. The cast and crew were very friendly and producer/director, Matthew Robinson, was a hard-working director who wanted everything to be as good as it could be.

I didn't have a great deal to do with the 'Grovers'. I knew them of course but I didn't have many scenes with them. Most of mine, in the first series, were with my wife and daughter.

Towards the end of the series I met Matthew in the canteen at the BBC Headquarters in Newcastle. At this point we still didn't know whether there'd be a second series. I told him that if there were, I'd do my own driving. Living in London I'd never had the need to drive and there are many actors like me who had never bothered to learn. Nowadays, actors are encouraged to multi-task. If you can act and sing, play an instrument and juggle, then you should be kept busy. Especially if you can do them all at the same time!

I should have learned to drive if only for work purposes. I went for a very good role some years after *Byker Grove*. The director was one I'd always wanted to work with. We had a great chat and I eventually got the part. When the script arrived, I was shocked to see that my first appearance had me driving very fast at Avonmouth Docks, Bristol, braking to a halt on the pier. I wouldn't fancy doing that even if I could drive. I phoned the production office and explained that I didn't drive. The director was furious. "Why didn't you say?"

"Well, I had no idea driving was involved. I'd not seen a script. If I'd known there was driving, I'd have admitted that I wasn't a driver. If I had been able to drive it would have been on my CV." A stand-in was used. I kept the part.

So here I was in a similar situation. I said to Matthew that between this first series and the next (if we went ahead with it) I'd have driving lessons and if driving was required, I'd do my own. Remember that the actress playing my wife was cast because she could drive. She (in the second series) has gone back to London, so any driving would have to be done by me (or a stand-in). Matthew didn't seem bothered. But I was determined.

Sometime later we got the exciting news that there was to be another series. Not only did children around the country understand what the Geordie kids were saying, they were impersonating the accent.

Before we all said our 'goodbyes' after series one, there was a big 'wrap' party. I happened to be sitting at one point next to Declan Donnelly who was playing Duncan in the series. He'd always been a polite lad and friendly. We chatted about the fact that he wanted to be an actor. I didn't want to put him off but I did say that I'd had a wonderful career as an actor but you have to go into it with your eyes open. I'd been lucky as I'd worked a lot and had not had to do any other work in between acting jobs. I was always fairly busy. But (oh my God, I really did say this to Dec), "Don't go in for it if you want fame and fortune!" Dec, of course, famously teamed up with fellow *Byker Grove* actor, Anthony McPartland, who I don't think I met on the series. He arrived later. So, the moral here is, don't take any notice of what I say!

Back to the driving. I booked myself into a two-week 'crash course' (Yes, I thought that was an unfortunate name, too!) where every day (with the same instructor) I'd go out for a drive. My instructor, Terri, was lovely but very firm. Bossy even! She explained many things and I'd always say, "But why do I do that?"

In the end she threw up her hands and said, "Look, Gordon, will you just do as I tell you. You'll make a good driver if you'd just stop asking all these questions. Just do as I say!" I did as she said and I was driving. It was dual control. In one of the early lessons when we were driving in very heavy traffic in north London, I was a bit panicky. "You are using the dual controls, aren't you?" She looked at me with a smile. "Nope. You're on your own!"

Driving on the busy North Circular road was terrifying with huge lorries looming overhead. Terri cleverly gave me directions to follow and, suddenly, we were driving gently through Epping Forest with the sun streaming through the trees. For the first time I could understand why people got pleasure from driving.

Terri was encouraging. My three-point turn wasn't a thing of beauty but she did think that I stood a good chance of passing the test. When the test date was announced, I'd have a couple of extra lessons with her (I should say at this point that many years before this, I'd had a few lessons so knew the basics).

So, I nervously waited for my test date. In the meantime, I went on a skiing trip… Ha-ha! You're ahead of me! Yes. Romania. My second day of skiing. I had my own skis but was hiring boots. The hut where the boots were kept was on a small hill. It was very icy. There was no sign of any gritters. I struggled up the slope with my skis over my shoulders. And slipped. And fell heavily. I don't know which hurt more, my elbow or my pride. My elbow was sore but I carried on skiing that morning. Lunch was back at the hotel. The first course was some meaty, steamy soup. I picked up my soupspoon and couldn't lift the spoon to my mouth. Somehow my arm had locked. I knew then that something was wrong.

Our guide was a smashing guy who whisked me off to the local hospital. It was rather Kafkaesque. We walked down very dark corridors (he explained that it was very hard to get light bulbs) and I could just make out people sitting and lying on the floor. Suddenly we arrived in a room with lots of people waiting. But Roman pushed me towards a large door. He knocked, said something and ushered me in.

I felt very uncomfortable jumping the queue but before I could object the doctor was speaking. He lay back in his leather swivel chair smoking a cigarette. He asked me what had happened. Roman explained. The doctor stubbed out his cigarette and gave my arm a cursory examination. Then he smiled and said what sounded like 'no fractura!'

I protested slightly to Roman, "But I am sure it *is* broken." The doctor had assured him that it wasn't broken but that I was to go somewhere in the hospital where I'd get the arm put into plaster and then, he advised, I should get back to the UK as quickly as possible and go at once to my local hospital!

In a very strange and smelly room, a woman, dressed all in black made a plaster for my arm. And fitted a sling. And that was it. I'd agreed with the friends I'd gone on holiday with that they'd take my skis back to London.

I couldn't get a flight back for a couple of days so I used the free days to sightsee, including a fascinating trip to Bucharest, with Roman being a perfect guide. Bucharest was only slowly getting back to normal after the horrifying regime of Ceauseścu. Bullet marks could still be seen defacing the walls.

I got back to London in one piece and presented myself at my local hospital, the Royal Free in Hampstead. The nurses there confirmed that I had indeed broken my arm. They did a wonderful job of fixing me up. If I'd left coming to see them any later, I might have lost the function that makes one twist the arm (turning a doorknob, using a tin opener, even playing the piano). Phew! I'd got to the Royal Free just in time.

All this meant three weeks with my arm in a sling. I could, of course, still work. Although I am right-handed and it was my right arm that was in a sling, I could still turn over the page of a script and I could even write. It was an odd handwriting, very different from my normal style but it was readable.

One of the first things that I had to do was postpone my driving test. I would be given another date. The new date for the driving test coincided with my mother being very ill. I was zipping up regularly to the northeast to see her in hospital and it was just too difficult concentrating on the test.

I cancelled the test for the final time. I went back to do the second series of *Byker Grove* and a stand-in drove for me. I knew that I could do the fairly simple driving that was required of me, but the insurance company wouldn't let me. Quite right too.

I had some wonderfully dramatic scenes in series two of *Byker Grove* including being beaten up at a squat where I was eventually pushed downstairs. Great stuff.

One thing that not many people know and I often forget myself, is that many years later, I went back into *Byker Grove*, playing another part. I knew none of the actors by then and I looked rather different.

For the new role I grew a moustache. I played a magistrate. It was only one episode but a lovely part. The storyline involved some Grover who had got into trouble. I was not up to speed with the series and just went in for my one day's filming. We filmed in a real magistrate's court but on a Saturday when it was closed.

Talking of court scenes, I was in an episode of *Kavanagh QC*, a series that starred John Thaw. It was also supposed to be set in a northeast court. I had a part in it but was also employed to teach the leading actress the Geordie accent. I think that you either have the facility for accents or you haven't and she admitted that she hadn't. Goodness knows why she had been cast. We spend quite a while together. I was behind the camera and also with her in the post-sync booth when she was voicing scenes she'd already filmed so that she could consult me before she did the scenes. She gave a moving performance but anyone in the northeast would know that she was not a Geordie, despite my best efforts.

Around this time I was approached by a Newcastle-based agent who wanted me to join him. He reckoned that there was so much work in the area it made sense to have an agent who was 'on the spot'.

One of the first jobs he put me up for was a film about the Knights of the Round Table. The director was an American Mormon and the film was being made with money from that organisation. I found the director rather brusque but the interview went well and I was offered the part of The Knight of the Torch.

I was picked up from my mother's flat on the first day of shooting and whisked to the location somewhere in the wilds of Northumberland. After getting into my costume (rather splendid) and getting made up, I was ushered with other 'knights' to the location where the filming was to take place. The assistant introduced me to a pleasant looking man who was standing beside a collection of horses.

He looked at the clipboard that he held in his hand and led me to a handsome, though very big, horse.

"This will be your horse," he said.

I looked horrified.

"What? But no-one said I had to ride a horse."

He looked perplexed and looked again at his clipboard. "Gordon Griffin. Knight of the Torch. Yes, this is your horse."

"But I don't ride."

"You have to. We're filming the sequence where the knights ride into the wood. You ride alongside King Arthur at the front of the procession holding up your flaming torch."

I protested: "But I don't ride. I'd have said so at the interview if they'd asked. I tried it once and it wasn't a success."

However, I felt I had no choice but to get onto the horse. I sat there awaiting instructions as other actors, with more confidence than I had, leapt onto their mounts.

My horse seemed particularly frisky. It started to wander off. I had no control over it. I called to the 'wrangler' or whatever he was called.

"My horse is wandering off! What do I do?"

He looked at me rather pathetically but then changed his look to one of sympathy. He came over and said, "OK, off you come." He helped me down to earth!

"There's no way you are getting on to that or any other horse. I wouldn't put a non-driver into a car and tell him to drive."

I was so relieved. But what now? I was supposed to be riding with King Arthur into the wood.

The director came over to find what the trouble was.

After he'd heard the 'wrangler' out, he turned to me, furious.

"Why didn't you say you couldn't ride at the interview?"

I answered truthfully: "You never asked me. If you'd asked me, I'd have said that I couldn't."

Then I had an idea.

"If we are supposed to be riding slowly into the wood, why don't I *walk* alongside the king holding the torch aloft?"

The director thought for a moment and then nodded. "Yes. We'll do that."

In the meantime, an extra, dressed in his fine knight's costume, climbed onto 'my' horse. He assured everyone that he was an experienced rider.

I must say that the image of all those actors on fine horses lined up in twos ready to shoot the scene, was most impressive.

The director kept looking anxiously at the lowering sky. He wanted this shot in the can before the rain came.

We were lined up in position. My torch was lit. I raised it high above my head and took my position beside the king, who looked magnificent on his splendid white horse.

"Action!"

The procession strolled slowly towards the entrance to the wood. It did look a magnificent sight, the splendidly dressed knights riding two-by-two as the light was fading. Suddenly there was a rustle and a neighing sound. I was aware that behind me there was a commotion.

"Cut!"

I turned around and was horrified to see the horses moving agitatedly and neighing in a panicked way. The flame of my torch had obviously spooked them. From amongst the frightened horses suddenly leapt 'my' horse with the extra on it. It galloped across the field with the terrified actor hanging on. We stared in horror. Eventually the actor managed to leap off and, even at a distance, we could see he'd fallen badly and wasn't moving.

We started to dash to his aid.

"Stay where you are!" yelled the director. "Get back into position. The light's going!"

The concussed actor was taken to hospital and was, I understand, kept in overnight. I just kept thinking that it could have been me.

It was decided to cut the torch and I was given a huge flag instead. I held this aloft instead of the torch. The horses behaved. The director got his shot and I must say it looked beautiful on the screen. But there were a lot of unhappy mutterings between the actors, concerned for our injured colleague.

I was in other scenes. The actual Round Table scene was filmed at Alnwick Castle and there was one sequence where we were filming outside the castle through the night. When you are freezing cold at three in the morning and you are doing an outdoor shoot, coffee is what you need to keep you warm and keep you going. Mormons don't drink coffee. None was allowed on the set.

Interestingly, when the film came out, on the cast-list at the end of the film, it credits me as playing The Knight of the Torch. I can imagine people watching the film thinking, "Where did the Knight of the Torch come into it!"

Around this time, I got a call from a London agent asking me to go along and meet the director and producer of a dramatised documentary called *Westminster on Trial* in the

Dispatches series. "They want to see you for the part of John Major!"

I was horrified. "But I look nothing LIKE John Major," I said.

"They want to see you. They saw your photograph in Spotlight."

"They saw my photograph and thought I looked like John Major?" I repeated.

I was assured that they did indeed want to see me for the part of the Prime Minister (as he was then).

The documentary was a transcript of the *Sale of Arms to Iraq* scandal and it dramatised the actual tribunal into the affair.

I remember thinking what a waste of time it was for me to be schlepping into the West End to be seen for a part I was dead wrong for.

The director and producer were very nice and charming. I was dreading that they'd ask me to read something. Major has a very distinctive voice, much impersonated, and I wasn't sure I'd be able to reproduce it. But more to the point, I didn't look like him.

They made it clear that they weren't necessarily looking for someone who looked or sounded exactly like Major which I thought was a bit odd. At that time he was just about the most recognisable person in the country.

It was a pleasant interview but I had no doubt that the part wasn't for me.

My hair was grey. When I got home, I combed it forward and found some large glasses and put them on and looked at myself in the mirror. Oh my God. I didn't look like him... and yet.

My agent phoned. "They want you to play the part!"

From then on, I watched about every film I could find of Major (this was pre-YouTube, of course) which wasn't easy. I watched *PM's Questions* on TV and I listened hard to try and get the voice right. Slowly, but surely, I was getting there. There was a particularly stiff arm movement he made. I worked on that. And then I had to learn the words exactly as written. His speeches to the tribunal were rather rambling and hesitant and sometimes didn't quite make sense. That didn't matter. I had to learn them word for word.

I was rather nervous at the first rehearsal in Hammersmith Town Hall where we eventually were to film. But no one laughed or said, "You're nothing like him!" and, in fact, at one point, the director (Oliver Horsbrugh) complimented me on my voice and gestures.

Margaret Thatcher was also called before the tribunal. She was to be played by the wonderful Maggie Steed. We got on famously from the start. She was delightful. Great fun. But on the day of the recording, I was on my way to the set (dressed and made up à la Major) when a door was flung open and there was Maggie Steed dressed to the nines as Maggie Thatcher. I backed against the wall as she strode down the corridor. She looked terrifying! And so scarily like the real Mrs T.

Two splendid actors played the barristers and they had so much to learn and, even though legitimately they could peep at their notes from time to time, their feat of learning was most impressive.

Those giving evidence to the enquiry included, as well as Mrs T and Mr Major, Michael Heseltine and various civil servants who, in fact, had quite a lot to say (more than Maggie and me).

The room was set out to look like the original enquiry room and someone had the brilliant idea of getting the courtroom artist, Priscilla Coleman, who during the actual enquiry drew pastel pictures of those involved which were shown on the television news, to do the same job at our 'mock' tribunal.

She kindly gave me my picture after the shoot. So I am the proud possessor of an original Priscilla Coleman and guess what? I look just like John Major! And indeed, when the programme was shown, I was amazed at how like the then Prime Minister I looked. Uncanny really.

There's a funny postscript to this. The producer had hired a large table at a local Italian restaurant and, of course, the bigwigs were there but not many of the cast. However,

Maggie Steed and I were invited. I am sure only because we played recognisable characters. We certainly didn't have the most to do! So, as well as having fun, I also got a very nice Italian meal and quite a lot of champagne!

Chapter 18

Over the years, I had had a lot of theatre experience. But once I started recording audiobooks, it became more difficult to commit. I was being booked ahead now and my diary was pretty full with recording dates. However, in the 1990s, I got a call to meet Mark Clements who was to become director of the Derby Playhouse, a fine rep theatre. The play was *And a Nightingale Sang* by CP Taylor. The play is set on Tyneside during the war and was the perfect part for me. 'Geordie' Stott is the head of a working-class Newcastle family so the play required an actor to play the dad who could do a Geordie accent. But on top of that, he had to play the piano. In the play, to avoid his nagging wife, he escapes to the parlour and plays the songs of the day (like the eponymous *A Nightingale Sang* in Berkeley Square). I do play the piano but am not keen to play in public, but in this play, Geordie wouldn't necessarily be a great pianist nor a great singer. It would be him singing and playing after all. I once saw a production of the play where the actor playing Geordie was a wonderful jazz pianist and when he played the songs from the show, he was dazzling. But it was ridiculous. There was no way that Geordie Stott would be that good.

I'd been used to playing young parts and Geordie Stott was my first real character part but I felt I could play him. Mark Clements obviously felt the same. I read a short scene from the play and was offered the role. "I am trusting you when you say you can play the piano," he said as I was leaving the audition.

Mark's production was wonderful. He'd assembled a marvellous ensemble and we all had a great time playing to packed houses.

In 2000, I got a call from my agent to say that the Bolton Octagon Theatre was planning a production of *A Nightingale Sang* and the director Kate Sinclair wanted to see me for the part of Geordie Stott. I must say that I liked the idea of playing the part again but I knew that I couldn't do it. I was booked to do a couple of audiobooks and also to cast *An Ideal Husband* for the English Theatre of Hamburg. I wasn't free.

Kate wouldn't take no for an answer. I'd explained that I wasn't available to do the play but she asked (via my agent) if we could at least meet. It seemed pointless but I reluctantly went to see her.

She showed me the set and told me that the mother (my wife in the play) was to be Rosalind Bailey, an actress I admired. We'd played husband and wife before in the TV series, *Andy Robson* and, according to Kate, Ros had recommended me for the part and she'd persuaded Kate to cast me.

When I heard that Ros was to play Ma Stott, I wavered. I wanted to do it. But what could I do? I said to Kate, with not much optimism, that I'd see what I could do and get back to her. Gill, who now ran Soundings, was marvellous. She rescheduled one of the books and the other went to another reader. I organised a friend, who had helped me with the casting on previous occasions, to cast the Oscar Wilde play. My agent contacted Kate. I was in!

Kate had assembled another wonderful authentically Geordie cast and everyone was very good but somehow, it didn't quite recapture the magic of the previous production. My brother drove from the northeast with my mother who, by now, was frail and not very well. It was the last time she was to see me onstage: the woman who had encouraged me to keep at it when others had said that I wouldn't be able to make it as an actor with a Geordie accent! I must say though, nothing would have stopped me whatever she'd thought, but knowing she was 'on my side' was a huge help. My brother too never once doubted that I could do it. I owe them both a lot.

Friends came up from London to see the show which was lovely especially as I realised that, if I was going to continue recording audiobooks, this could prove to be my last appearance on a stage.

I could still carry on doing my talks, of course. They only required an afternoon or an evening, except during Make a Noise in Libraries fortnight when I could be charging around doing up to five or six a week.

My friend, the French singer Françoise Geller, had asked me join her doing concerts and cabaret and when I was free, I was happy to oblige especially when I was recording a lot of books. I didn't mind where we performed. I enjoyed the singing and having an audience to perform to. Our repertoire was the American songbook and songs from the shows. We played Friendship Clubs and at weddings and birthdays and even a memorable gig at the five-star Landmark Hotel near Baker Street in London.

When we had a middle-aged or elderly audience, I included in the show my Jessie Matthews medley. Sadly, a lot of younger people don't know of Jessie. But older people do. I'd arranged three of her hit songs that segued from one to the other with only a couple of bars between each song. (Such wonderful songs, too: *My Heart Stood Still, Dancing on the Ceiling* and, of course, her signature tune, *Over My Shoulder*).

At one performance, I'd just finished the first song (*My Heart Stood Still*) when an elderly man got to his feet. I was rather surprised to be getting a standing ovation so early in the medley. He called out at the top of his voice, "Does anyone know how to open these windows? It's bloody hot in here!"

My mum tried to organise her trips to stay with me so that she could see me and Françoise performing together. We did solo numbers but mostly we sang together and we certainly had a rapport onstage.

One day we were performing at some club in Central London. My mum was sitting, all smiles, on the front row. Françoise and I were mid-number when the elderly lady beside my mum leant into her and told her conspiratorially, "They're married, you know."

My mother put her right. "No," she assured her, "They are just good friends. They're not married."

The other woman looked at my mother rather pityingly. "They are married," she insisted. "I know it for it for a fact!"

My mother smiled at her. "They work well together, don't they? But they are not married. He's my son."

The woman looked at my mother and shook her head. "I don't care if he is your son. They *are* married!"

My mother gave up. "If you insist," she said.

My auditions and interviews dwindled as it became clear my audiobook work prevented me having time to do any other work. It was taking over. More and more companies were starting up and it was gratifying that they were asking me to record for them. I was happy to be so busy.

Eventually, I was working flat out. My schedule was crazy. I spend hours on trains commuting to the studios, a lot of them being out of London. That suited me fine as I was able to do my work on the trains.

I found that the audiobooks were taking over a chunk of my life. I always had two or three books lined up to be prepared and recorded. Often more. It meant my bedtime reading was whatever book I was preparing. My poolside reading on holiday was a book that I was to record. On the underground. On buses. In the garden. I was always reading with a pencil in my hand to mark the scripts.

But it was my choice. I enjoyed it. Friends would say, "You are working too hard," but I ignored them. I knew that I thrived on the work although I did sometimes look at my schedule and think, *Oh, goodness. How am I going to do all these books?* but I always did. And I was always prepared.

I know readers who busk it. Skim read. I read an interview with a well-known reader who said that he had so many books to record that he couldn't actually read them all before he went into the studio. I was shocked by that. He reckoned that he was a good sight-reader and could get through a book without having read it. I think that is a high-risk strategy and not to be recommended. I too am a good sight-reader. If someone handed me a book I'd not read before and said, "Let's record it now without you looking at it first", I know that I could. But my point is that there are so many traps to recording in that way. And the recording is never going to be as good as if you'd prepared. If you have done your homework, then you know the characters, their voices, where the plot is leading. To sight-read means that you have no signposts. You rely on instinct. Fine but not infallible.

There are so many examples of actors who didn't prepare and came a cropper. Not long ago, a well-known and much-loved actor who prided himself on being a good sight-reader, was recording a book out of London. He'd skim read it, he said, but on the second day of recording towards the end of the session, it was realised that one of the main characters who he had been reading in his own voice (i.e. an English accent) was, in fact, an American. What to do? Go back to the beginning and 'drop in' re-recordings of all the American's dialogue. The trouble was there was so much of it and it was decided that it'd be simpler just to record the whole book again. So, they started again. Unfortunately, the reader who was to record a book the following day in the same studio, was already on the train heading north. He was sent home. Chaos and frustration because the famous reader hadn't prepared.

You really have to read every word. Recently, I had a book set in a small town in Yorkshire. Fairly early on, we are introduced to the couple who run the local pub. They've run it for some years and all the locals know them. As I was reading it through, I had decided in my head to give them quite strong Yorkshire accents. However, later in the story, when they are both interviewed by the police, it's noted that both the landlord and his wife were born and brought up in Birmingham and still retained a strong Midlands accent!

There are so many examples of this and it's just not worth taking the risk of not thoroughly reading the book. Reading and preparing. Preparation is all.

So, the lad from the northeast had made it. The journey has been an interesting one and I certainly hadn't planned to record so many books. But I do recall, as a drama student, saying that it was my ambition to work. To make a living from being an actor, however that was achieved. And I have.

I remember those early days as a shy actor (long before emails and the internet) when to get an audition, I'd have to phone up the producers or casting directors myself. In one sense it was easier then. You usually got to speak to whoever you were phoning. And BBC producers and casting directors too would set aside time when they weren't busy, to give general auditions to actors. I was cast in a number of television roles in this way.

It was never my plan to break records recording so many books. Not at all. I am not trying to record more than anyone else. In fact the reason that I know how many books I have recorded is all down to a wonderful old radio stalwart, Garard Green. I was doing a radio play with him and he casually asked me about the 'talking books' I'd recently started to record.

"How many have you done?" he asked.

I thought about it. "Oh, about eight or nine."

He looked surprised. "You don't know? But my dear boy, you must keep a record!"

So when I went home that evening, I made a list of the books I had recorded and every time I recorded another, I added it to the list. And when I had my first website, I put the list onto it. And continued to add new titles. Now, three to four websites later, there is the list. If I hadn't taken Garard's advice, I am sure that I'd not have believed that I'd recorded so many books!

But I love the work and it's the perfect job for an actor. It's like being in a radio play where you are the narrator and you get to play all the parts, you're the director and producer and you're the casting director too! And that's why it was a bit annoying when I was being interviewed once, on a record show on radio, by a presenter who kept on saying, between records, "We have here in the studio Gordon Griffin, who used to be an actor but who now records audiobooks!" After he'd said it a third time, I had to interrupt him. "Actually, I am still an actor!"

Recording books is a commitment. My nephew once, half-jokingly, told me that he envied me my cushy job. All I had to do was to sit at a microphone all day and tell stories! In one sense he was right because by the time you get to the studio the preparation is done. All you have to do then is put into practice what you've prepared.

Part Three
Staying There

Chapter 19

Amazingly, the question I am asked most, is whether I have to read the book I am recording beforehand! This shows that people don't even think of the process of recording an audiobook. It's the fact that we don't have to learn the words, I suppose, that makes people think it's quite easy. Or maybe they think that the reader just goes to the studio, picks up his script and records. Actually, I heard of a well-known actor who arrived at a studio to record his first audiobook. The producer greeted him, welcomed him to the studio and asked if he'd enjoyed the book. The actor ferreted in his bag and brought out the sealed envelope with the script still in it! It hadn't been opened. He clearly thought you worked in the studio a chapter at a time. He'd been booked for three days. It took him over two weeks!

So, yes, you read the book beforehand at least once. If it's a complicated book like Andrew Hodge's dense biography of Alan Turin (*Alan Turin – the Enigma*) that I recorded some years ago, I reread some sections numerous times. I had to understand what I was saying and sometimes that meant a lot of extra work. It felt as though I was doing research for a PhD!

I have recorded audiobooks for over thirty years and I have seen the industry change so much. Everything is digital now, which makes recording smoother and easier for everyone. The editors no longer have to cut up tape! Nowadays, we mostly record from iPads, so the book I am to record is sent to me in a file which I download into an app called iAnnotate which allows me to mark up my scripts, something I find invaluable. When I used to record from photocopied pages, I would make copious notes for myself: descriptions of characters, symbols that told me if a line was funny or sad, and, above all, I'd underline relevant words. This way you'll make sense and make fewer mistakes.

On the iPad, I use the same hieroglyphics, only there's not quite so much space so I have to be more economical. I have listened to readers where you know that they have no idea where the sentence they are reading is going. If you underline the relevant words, you won't have this problem.

Sometimes, it's even necessary to re-punctuate. Two great writers that I've recorded, Hilary Mantel and Peter Carey, both have rather eccentric punctuation so I adapted it to suit me; I would change a semicolon to a comma, say, or a colon to a full stop, to make the narration flow more easily when being read aloud. Most modern writers use commas sparingly and that's a great help for narrators. Too many commas can act like a tripwire ready to catch out the unprepared narrator.

When I am prepping, I hear the voices I plan to use in my head. Sometimes, I'll read sections allowed. Rehearse the various voices. I'll mark the script with a word or two to remind me of the quality of the voice. One word can give me the clue. If I have written 'Sinden' in the margin, for example, the voice will be deep and rich and resonant or if I write 'Gielgud', the voice will be elegant and light. I don't mean, of course, that I impersonate Donald Sinden or John Gielgud, but it gives me an instant clue.

If you practise, you'll not be fazed by having to do multiple voices. I once had a scene to read where a Belfast woman was having a blazing row with an Italian taxi-driver. Another time, it was a suspect being interrogated by two policemen who acted like a double act, speaking faster and faster to intimidate their victim. One cop was a rough diamond with a gruff London accent and the other was described as having a high-pitched Birmingham accent. To make that work, I needed a lot of concentration.

I try not to go 'over the top' with the voices. I try to be subtle. If the character is described as Scottish, it doesn't mean he has to sound like Billy Connolly!

And you have to be prepared to do every accent under the sun. Writers don't always make it easy though. I have a facility for accents but sometimes I am defeated. I recorded one book about the adventures of a vet who is the narrator of the book. At one point he is doing his surgery when a rather elegant lady walks in. He tells us, "From the moment she started speaking, I knew she was from Dumfries!" The only consolation there was that I asked an actress friend to help. She is Scottish, born and bred, but she couldn't. "I wouldn't know where to begin," she said.

If I have Norwegian to speak in a book, I'll find a Norwegian. If a character is Basque, then, somehow, I'll need to track down a Basque speaker. I have had to do huge chunks of Swahili and, rather surprisingly, I got a review that praised my perfect Hungarian! Not a language I know but one I had to learn for a recording. I once recorded a book that had chunks of Russian in it. I spent days (and nights) going over the words. It was worth the effort because when I got to the studio the words tripped off my tongue. I know some readers rely on the producers to do the research and sometimes are only handed the pronunciations when they arrive at the studio. That wouldn't work for me, as I'd need to be really secure, and that takes time.

Some years ago, I had a book with quite a few Vietnamese phrases in it. I was wondering who to contact: the tourist office, the embassy? Then I remembered that there was a Vietnamese restaurant up the road not far from where I live. I went in to order a take-away. While I was waiting, I asked the manager if there was anyone there who spoke Vietnamese.

"No one," he said and disappeared downstairs with my order to where the kitchen was.

Oh well, I would at least have a nice meal.

Suddenly, he was back with a big grin on his face. He was followed by a wizened old man wearing a non-too-clean white chef's jacket.

The manager ushered the older man over to my table. "He speak Vietnamese. I forgot. Assistant chef."

He sat down beside me and I showed him the first phrase in the book that I needed to know how to say. He looked blank. Of course, he did! It was written in English in an approximation of the actual Vietnamese language. I had a brainwave. I told him the context and read what was written with conviction. His face lit up.

"Ah, yes… You say…"

And so, we got through the words. Nowadays, of course, the internet is very helpful. When I was recording the autobiography of Chris Bonington, *Ascent*, I was daunted by the massive list of words to check. Snowdonian villages, Gaelic ridges, Tibetan passes. Amazingly, with my producer's help, we found most of them online. I watched loads of YouTube films of Bonington's expeditions, hoping that someone would say the name I was, at that time, searching for.

Once (pre-internet), I recorded a book that had two characters speaking Cornish. I don't mean the Cornish accent but the actual language. I had a brainwave. I found the telephone number of the main public library in Penzance. I rang the number and said rather plaintively to the lady who replied, "Do you know anyone who speaks Cornish?" It was a long shot but I'd struck gold.

She replied, "Yes. I do. Well, at least I am learning it!"

She was able to not only translate the words (it turned out to be *The Lord's Prayer*) but also to give me the pronunciations.

Only once did I come to a dead end. Again, this was before the internet. I recorded a series of delightful books about a Mallorcan policeman called Enrique Àlvarez. What I didn't realise then, but know now all these years later, was that someone like Àlvarez would speak Mallorquin, a Catalan dialect. Not Spanish.

This particular story concerned a rare mushroom-like fungus that grows on the island. I can't now recall its name, although I remember it being (to me) unpronounceable. The point was that this fungus is highly poisonous and was being chopped up and used in food by some unscrupulous person to kill his enemies. The word appeared countless times. It was a critical part of the plot. It was vital I got the pronunciation correct!

I phoned the Spanish tourist office where a rather brusque man told me that the world was Catalan and therefore had nothing to do with Spanish!

I next phoned a Spanish friend who worked in the catering industry in Mallorca. He didn't know the word either but he gave me the phone number of a friend of his who was from Palma and who worked for a travel company. Perfect!

Another call to Mallorca. The friend was charming and apologetic. He couldn't help. He'd not heard of this rare fungus.

Now what? Well, there was only one more thing I could think of. I needed to speak to the writer of the book, Roderic Jeffries Although English, Jeffries lives in Mallorca so it involved yet another call to the island.

I explained who I was and that I recorded his books. I was able to say truthfully how much I enjoyed them. He was very courteous. He'd enjoyed my recordings. So, we were off to a good start.

I reminded him of the plot of the book that I was about to record and then spelled out the word I needed to pronounce.

My pen was poised, the receiver clamped to my ear. "How do you say it?" I asked.

"I have no idea," he answered. "I made it up!"

Chapter 20

The whole recording industry has changed so much. The internet has been such a boon. Apart from not having to deal with pages of paper, using the iPad means you can make the font bigger or smaller. You don't even need a light in the studio as the screen is illuminated and perhaps, most importantly, you don't have to worry about making a noise as you turn over a page.

The internet has been so useful in many ways. I used to spend hours in the library checking pronunciations from the multi-volume Oxford dictionary there. Now I can find most pronunciations online. But one has to use pronunciation sites with care. The major dictionary sites are useful but some sites are unreliable and you often need to double check. More than once I have checked the pronunciation of a particular word only to find that two 'reliable' sources pronounce it differently. When I was preparing Homer's Odyssey there were about six different pronunciation variations for each of the character's names depending on which site you looked at.

But the internet is a boon. If I have an audition for a commercial, say, my agent simply emails me the details whereas before she'd have had to phone me. And in my role of casting director, it has been invaluable. I can even send contracts and scripts by email instead of queuing up at a post-office – if you can find one! I can book actors by email too. It's all so much easier.

One really has to keep up. At the monthly meeting of my local Equity (trade union) branch, I was astonished by an older actor who complained that the Newsletter was no longer send by post. "But," the chairman explained, "It's online."

The actor rather proudly announced, "Well, I don't have a computer." More fool him.

The next big thing in the world of audiobooks is going to be home-recording. In the US, most narrators record from home and already here it's becoming more and more accepted. As more audiobooks are recorded, there aren't always enough studios to go around, so recording from home is encouraged. Of course, it necessitates having somewhere in your home that's soundproofed but aside from that, all you need is a very good microphone. Recording from home would be a much more solitary experience and as well as telling the story, you'd have to be listening for any mistakes. But I am sure my first self-recorded book will happen in the not too distant future[*].

One of the pleasures of recording in a studio is that you can concentrate completely on telling the story. You don't have to listen for mistakes as someone else is doing that for you. When recording from home you'd have to tell the story as before but part of your brain has to be listening to what you're saying and picking up any misreading.

And I also enjoy the idea of 'going to work', of socialising, of meeting other people. Recording from home is more solitary. I heard of one reader who records from home. Before he starts recording for the day, he walks around the block. When he's finished, he takes himself for another walk. That 'getting out the house' feeling I completely understand.

I was once part of an online forum for audiobook narrators who record from home. They were able to ask advice of other readers. I remember that one reader wanted to know if anyone had advice for her on how to deal with her cat. She loved to record with the cat on her knee but unfortunately, this cat tended to purr a lot. I didn't stay long as a member of this forum.

A friend of mine was editing an audiobook that had been recorded at the reader's home in rural France. My friend had a very difficult time editing out the chirruping birdsong in the background. So recording from home can have its problems.

---

[*] In March 2020, during lockdown, I recorded the first of a number of books at home.

But on the other hand, some home (or 'remote') studios can be better than conventional studios. More and more readers are recognising that it's not such a complicated process and publishers like the fact that home recording saves them money!

At least when recording from home you'd be more relaxed, I'd imagine, and being relaxed is essential when recording a book. So, wear clothes that are comfortable. Never wear leather or starched shirts or dangling jewellery. And make sure your watch doesn't tick! The microphones are so sensitive they pick up any extraneous noise.

Once, in the studio next to me was one of the female stars of *Coronation Street* recording a book about the series. The engineers were baffled by a crackling sound that was coming through while she was reading. Eventually, it was decided that somehow her over-lacquered hair was causing the problem. Sounds unlikely to me, but that's what the engineer decided.

But I am sure that whether one records at home or in a studio, it's still just you and the microphone. You tell the story; you draw in the listeners whether you're in a posh Soho studio or your soundproofed back bedroom!

But, I guess, the point is that I just love telling stories. I recognise that it's a particular skill. I think that some actors aren't successful at it. It need not have anything to do with their acting ability. I read not long ago Finty Williams (a fine narrator) saying that her mother just couldn't do it. I think everyone will agree that her mother, Judi Dench, is a wonderful actor. But it's true that some actors who narrate want to 'act', to 'perform'. That's not it at all. It's not about performing to an audience of listeners. Rather, it's you (the narrator) saying "Come with me. Listen. I have this amazing story to tell you". You are bringing the listeners to you. Drawing them in. At least that is the plan. I know some narrators who show off by giving each character a distinctive voice. That's not it either. It's a subtler skill than that. If someone is listening to a recording of mine and they say "I like the way he's doing that voice", I have failed. The listener should be listening to the story and not how I am telling it.

One of my favourite reviews mentioned that when I read, I became anonymous, I 'disappeared'. That's what I am aiming for. Gordon Griffin disappears and the writer takes over.

Another thing that's worth mentioning is that when you are reading something, you *see* the word and know its meaning. If you are only *hearing* that same word it can have a different effect.

I recorded a book where there was a battle going on. Two people were involved in hand-to-hand combat with long-swords. In the novel it says that one of them 'feinted'. Someone listening might have heard 'fainted' and think, "Well, he's obviously lost that fight, then." So somehow that narrator has to describe what's happening in such a way that the listener gets the author's meaning. Not easy. A common example that occurs in period novels is the word 'gait'. "I recognised the parson's gait" could be misunderstood by the listener. I think the most ambiguous that I've had to record was in a Catherine Cookson novel where a young lady, having a tantrum, throws herself onto the pouffe. Ouch!

I once had to say the line, "He was so addicted to golf that he liked to get in a hole before breakfast!" We all know what the writer means but it would have helped if he'd written the sentence in a less ambiguous way.

A really good narrator (by certain inflections) should be able to differentiate between someone wearing 'a Deep Purple T-shirt' (the rock band) and a 'deep purple' T-shirt (the colour) or between a French teacher (a teacher from France) and a French teacher (someone who teaches French). Or a camp doctor (a medical man attached to a military establishment) and a camp doctor (a fey medical man!).

Another challenge is in a whodunit where the murderer appears long before he/she is unmasked. Of course, the writer doesn't identify them but may have them talking. I know it's the murderer (I've read the book) but I don't want the listener to know yet. I can't cheat but somehow, I have to disguise the voice enough so as not to give the game away. Once I used a nervous, whispered voice. But it can be tricky.

When I am recording a biography or autobiography, I try to listen to any recording of that person. It's not so easy if the subject is Nelson! But when I recorded Bruce Forsyth's memoir, I knew that it would be wrong to do an impersonation, but I needed to somehow convey the essence of his voice. It was the same when recording Keith Floyd's autobiography. I watched lots of his TV programmes and endeavoured to capture the mellifluous quality that his voice had.

It's a big responsibility. I can't stress enough that the most important person in the process is the writer. That must never be forgotten. The narrator is just the conduit. We always have to serve the writer!

Recording books is a great job for an actor. It's thrilling when the words come off the page. One can almost sit back, and the characters take over and the story flows along nicely. Magic happens. It's a wonderful feeling. And this applies whether it's a novel or a non-fiction book. You still tell the story, bring the listener into the world you're describing whether it is Chris Bonington climbing a mountain, Alan Turin cracking a code or a Geordie miner trudging home after a long day 'down the pit'.

And the same rule applies to non-fiction books and autobiography – tell the story.

Preparation is very important. If I don't have time to 'do the prep' I don't accept the book. The trouble is that I have a reputation for always being well prepared. One producer told me that if they have a very difficult book requiring lots of research, he'll say, "Get Gordon!" I replied, that that's all very well. But sometimes I am happy to record a nice little thriller set in Yorkshire. If I had to record long and complex books all the time, I'd go crazy!

But if you've prepared well, you'll make fewer mistakes. But making a mistake, stumbling over the odd word, is not a hanging offence. The secret is not to get fazed by it. I have known of readers who get into such a state when they make a mistake, that they get thrown and that makes things worse. It's true that if you are sailing through a book, getting into the book's rhythm and then you have to stop, that rhythm is broken and you'll make a few more mistakes before you get back into the rhythm again. It's important not to get thrown, though. Everyone makes mistakes

The great thing about being a professional storyteller is that, as long as your voice has the vocal energy, you can carry on, whatever your age.

I was recording a book at the RNIB when a very elderly man shuffled into the green room. I thought, *He can't be a reader.* But when he left the room, I asked one of the producers. The producer told me that he was indeed a reader and he mentioned a very well-established radio actor who has been around for years. He also told me how wonderful he still was at recording books. He was still working. His voice (even though he was well into his eighties) was still in good nick. I was thrilled and encouraged. In my own case, I'll go on until I decide that my voice can't cope any more or until I'm stopped being asked to record. At that point, I will happily hang up my headphones.

Telling stories has been a tradition for as long as there have been people to tell them. I am proud and happy to have been a part of that tradition.

My diary is as busy as ever. Lots of different books to record. Modern thrillers, classic novels, autobiographies. I love the variety. I love not knowing what is the next book I will be asked to record, Homer or Gogol or Dickens. A history of the world. The life of a famous writer. Or murder and mayhem in Morecambe. Bring 'em on!

And what's next? Ah, well… that's another story!

Postscript

I knew someone who had an important job at Buckingham Palace.

I was having dinner with him and his wife. I'd just told them about the MBE.

"It won't be the Queen," he said. "It's too long a time for her to stand. About an hour and a half. You'll get Prince Charles, Prince William or the Princess Royal."

I was just so thrilled and astonished that I was getting the award that in one sense it didn't really matter who presented it to me. But naturally it would have been very special if it had been Her Majesty.

On Tuesday November 7th I was in the beautiful gallery at Buckingham Palace awaiting the big event. You could feel the nervousness in the air. We recipients were given bottled water but I didn't want to drink too much. A uniformed gentleman with a dazzling array of medals was standing by a table on which were a lot of brochures.

I approached him.

"Excuse me, but do you know who is officiating today?" I asked him.

He smiled. "The Queen."

I had to stop myself from saying, "No it's not the Queen. I have it on good authority…"

He handed me a brochure. Sure enough, on the front it confirmed that the Queen was presenting the awards.

I was thrilled (it was only the second time she'd officiated that year apparently – and it was November!) but nervous. I now had to remember the protocol that I hadn't thought I'd need. When to say "Your Majesty" and when to say 'Ma'am' (to rhyme with 'jam'). A very jolly man rehearsed us walking backwards.

It was all so unreal. I walked into that magnificently vast room filled with beautifully dressed guests and with a small orchestra playing show tunes on a balcony overlooking the room. And there she was. The Queen.

It was all a bit of a haze. But we talked about audiobooks and I told her that I'd recorded nearly 800. I added, 'that's quite a lot of talking' which apparently made her laugh. I don't remember this but my family and friends who were there told me afterwards that she had indeed laughed at something I had said,

In my nervousness I forgot all the protocols except that I did say, "Thank you Ma'am" (to rhyme with jam!) after she'd shaken my hand. And just in time I remembered the backward walk.

She was so charming and seemed interested. But I just kept thinking "Is this really happening. To me!"

I think it really hit home when I saw the photographs posted later that day on the Buckingham Palace website. And there I was in three photographs. Me with the Queen. For the first time it really registered. There was the proof. It really had happened to me. I now had the photos to prove it. And the MBE!

I recalled that little lad growing up on Tyneside, who so much wanted to be an actor, but having a Geordie accent and coming from the background he came from, it was not a promising start. And, of course, that ambitious little boy was me. More than one person told me that it was a dream that wouldn't/couldn't come true. I wouldn't make it. Well, I DID make it.

Not that getting the honour was proof. To be respected by my peers was much more important. But to the wider world, this was recognition indeed.

The audio industry has come such a long way. No longer do people say, "Oh, you record books for the blind," in a rather disparaging way as though it wasn't a proper job. I know of actors who didn't want to do this work; who didn't regard it as a job at all. How things have changed. Now, to quote Ira Gershwin, "They're fighting to get in!" Actors now are queuing up to record audiobooks.

****

People ask me still, "How can I get into this world of audiobooks?" And my honest answer, although I can give them tips and hints, is that I don't know. It's something I have always done! I got my foot in the door early on. And that foot is still there. I am not complaisant. Not at all. When I am booked to record a book, I am still thrilled to be asked, even though, as I write this, I am heading for my 900th.

Lucky me! Somehow, I landed the perfect job. And I am still doing it! I think of that shy Geordie lad who, all those years ago, was so desperate to become an actor. I suspect he's somewhere inside me still… and he's probably smiling!

AND FINALLY… When I first wrote this book, I had resisted recording from home but then Covid hit and it was clear that, because of the restrictions, most studios had shut up shop during lockdown. If I wanted to continue recording, I'd need to bite the bullet and record remotely from home. I had set up a recording booth and after research I had invested in a very good microphone. My bedroom was the quietest room in the house and because of Covid, there were very few planes flying overhead. I made a demo-recording and sent it to the studios I normally worked for and was surprised but pleased that most were happy with the quality of my demo. I went on to record about fifteen titles at home. I didn't really enjoy it. What I love about recording in a studio is that someone else is listening for mistakes and I can concentrate on telling the story. Now, here I was having to listen to myself. And as I was listening for errors, I wasn't able to concentrate 100% on my reading. And editing was something I never really got the hang of, and when studios reopened, I was first in the queue! Many of my colleagues love the freedom of recording from home and I have, since lockdown, recorded a few titles in my bedroom. But given the choice, I'd always choose the studio environment.

I'd been asked in the past to run workshops for actors who wanted to record audiobooks. I usually resisted the offers as I'd always worked instinctively. I had no rules. I just did it. But it was suggested that for this book I include a section about the studio experience and how it is that I prepare a book for recording. For the first time I had to analyse what it was that I do. The revelation was that I had so much to say, so much to impart. So when I was next asked to host workshops, I responded enthusiastically. I really enjoy passing on my knowledge and working with actors, and I am happy to say these sessions are successful and ongoing. And the marvellous feedback encourages me to schedule more. Even as I head towards a thousand audiobook recordings, I am never complaisant and I can still be excited by telling a great story (whether fiction or nonfiction). And I love the variety. Not long ago, within a few weeks of each other, I recorded Dostoyevsky's *The Idiot* and Thomas Hardy's masterpiece *The Mayor of Casterbridge* followed by a history of humans and the autobiography of Bernard Cribbins! I rest my case! Lucky me!

Not long ago, I was asked by a publishing house to write some tips and advice for new narrators hoping to record audiobooks. This is what I rattled off. Apologies if some of this advice is already to be found in the main body of the book.

ADVICE TO NEW AUDIOBOOK NARRATORS FROM AN OLD STAGER

Preparation! Preparation! Preparation! The most important words you will need to know. There is no such thing as too much preparation! I think that people who have not recorded books think that as you are READING, there's not a great deal of work to do. Wrong!

You need to read the book (all of it) at least once. If there are difficult passages, you'll need to read them more than once.

NEVER skim read, however good at sight-reading you are. There are too many examples of narrators who missed a vital character note by not reading every word. One such example is of a well-known and busy actor who admitted that he skim-read this particular book. The recording was going well. On his final day, he came across a sentence that he'd skipped when he was preparing the book. It described how the main character in the story was American! He'd been reading it with an English accent. Because it was the main character in the book, there was no choice but to start the recording again. Three wasted days. But worse. The narrator, who was due to record in that same studio the next day (the studio wasn't in

London), was sent home and told to return in a couple of days' time! All because the original actor hadn't read the book properly. And there are many examples of this.

Mark up your script. This honestly helps. Underline the important words in a sentence; if you need to, re-punctuate to help you when reading. Some books, especially older ones, are a minefield with their old-type punctuation. I guarantee that if you mark up your script in this way, you will make fewer mistakes. It's not the end of the world, incidentally, to make a mistake. But most books have their own rhythm and every time you have to stop because of mistake, you have to get back into the rhythm again. That's why it often happens that if you make a mistake, you make three or four around the same time until you get back into the rhythm again. Don't get fazed or thrown if you make a mistake. Keep the momentum of the book in your head. Don't have a big discussion about the mistake. Keep calm and carry on!

Check the pronunciation of words you don't know. If you are even 90% sure of how a word is pronounced, check it anyway. You might be wrong. There are many ways to find correct pronunciations online. But use sites like The Oxford Dictionary of English. Don't use US dictionaries if you're checking pronunciations for a book that requires British English. Some pronouncing sites are not reliable so double check if you're not sure. I also have a hard-backed pronouncing dictionary that I have used since pre-digital days. It gives the phonetic pronunciations of the words, not the meanings but I find it an invaluable backup.

Place-names are particularly important to get right. You may think that if you guess the name of a village in North Wales or a town in Uzbekistan, no one will know. Someone WILL! Get it right. Best of all is to find a native speaker if you have some foreign language words to pronounce. Or phone the country's tourist office. ALWAYS check though. I was recording a Melvyn Bragg book and in it was the name of a Cumbrian river. There was only one way it could be pronounced, so I thought. I'd not need to check. But it niggled me. I couldn't find it online so I phoned the council offices of a nearby town. Thank goodness, I did. The river was not pronounced as I had guessed! Phew! It's always worth checking even if you were right and it's only confirmation of that.

No one can do all accents but to record audiobooks, you need a good ear. Accents can be subtly done. No need to 'go overboard' unless the writer states that the accent is very strong. But if, for example, you feel insecure about Geordie, and the main character in the book is Geordie, don't accept the book!

Preparation can take a long time. Sometimes (I am thinking of writers like Patrick O'Brian or Dorothy Dunnett or the Alan Turning biography I recorded a couple of years ago), and some non-fiction books, preparation can take much longer than the recording. If you don't have enough time to prep a book – again, don't accept it. You have to find the time to do the research and preparation fully. You may have days free in your diary to RECORD a book but you must make sure that you have plenty of time before that to PREPARE it. If you haven't, say no. If you say yes, your first book may be your last!

Read sections aloud. Hear how the main characters sound, not just in your head. Make notes on your script of the description of the characters' voices (maybe in the space between chapters), so that you know which characters are coming up so you are prepared for them.

Your first audiobook can be daunting but if you are prepared and know your book well, you'll be fine. Get comfortable. Take a deep breath and… tell the story.

And, this is a very important note! You are there to tell the story. Actors sometimes come a cropper because they want to ACT, to PERFORM. No, this is not performing to a large audience but rather telling a story to someone listening to it. It's a subtle skill. All characters (especially the very small roles) don't have to have specific voices. As long as the listener can understand what's going on and can differentiate between the characters. If you are a male reader, any female voices should be done subtly. There's not a great deal of difference between male and female voices. Lighten your voice for a female voice. Likewise, a deep gruff voice from a female narrator doing a male role also sounds wrong. Experiment until you find a voice that's real.

Don't show off with clever voices. With some narrators, it's all about them showing how clever and versatile they are. No. This is about serving the writer. It's not about YOU, the narrator. If someone is listening to one of my books and they say "I love the way he does that voice," then I have failed. They should be listening the story, not how I am telling it.

And if you don't like a book or its characters? It's irrelevant what you think. You are serving the writer. If you find the main man, say, insufferable and pompous but the writer has written him as charming and charismatic, then charming and charismatic he has to be!

There is, on the one hand, the writer and on the other hand, the listener, and between is... you. That's a huge responsibility. Don't forget that the writer is the most important person in the process.

Whatever the book is, you have to give it your best shot, make it real, even if you find the dialogue is UNREAL. Whether it's The Mill on the Floss or Mills and Boon, both have to be made to come alive in a real way.

So tell the story. Be subtle, except where the writer wants you not to be.

One of my favourite reviews said, "Gordon Griffin is anonymous... he disappears." Perfect. THAT is what I am trying to achieve. The story always has to come first.

Keep calm. PREPARE. And go for it.

Good luck!